CHASING FREEDOM

CHASING FREEDOM

ELLA MIRIAM

Copyright © 2015 Chasing Freedom Press
Published by Chasing Freedom Press

Designed by Vince Pannullo
Edited by Patti Spencer
Printed in the United States of America by RJ Communications.

Library of Congress Control Number: 2015942621

ISBN: 978-0-578-16437-3

To my children Anat, Jacob,

and Natalie, and to all my grandchildren

with love

The heritage of the past

is the seed that brings forth

the harvest of the future

—*Wendell Phillips, abolitionist*

CONTENTS

PART THREE: AMERICA

PREFACE

Sarah Lenahan

Mrs. Dean English 12 Honors A# March, 2012

IF

If you can say goodbye to your mother and father
To give a better life to your daughter,
If you can escape your home country
Because it strips away your freedom
And know when to take a risk
And fully commit.
If you can overcome the loss of your true love
And never hold on to a grudge.
If you can learn to start over
And accept that life is not fair,
If you can take in your challenges
And find an opportunity to strive,
If you can appreciate the little things in life
While admiring the greatest,
If you can put your famous ambitions aside
And choose to use your talent in only the classroom,
If you can love unconditionally
Those who do not share your blood,
If you can become a best friend to someone's child,
While still being a mother to your own,
And fully enrich the lives of others
With just one simple object,
If you can make music with your fingers
And memories with your heart,
If you can answer a deep question in only one word,
If you can be honest and critique,
But be loving and encouraging all the while,
If you can inspire an audience greater than a preacher,
Then you can be like Ella Miriam, my piano teacher.

ACKNOWLEDGEMENTS

I express my sincere appreciation to my family and friends for encouraging me to put into writing the stories of ordinary people from previous generations.

This is my own recollection and interpretation of the personal stories and historical events that have occurred in my family. The episodes of this book were either witnessed by me, lived by me or told to me by other family members or close friends. I relied exclusively on my own memory and was pleasantly surprised by the very curious and positive reception of those who heard these stories.

My sense is that this is a very timely book, especially considering the passage of history and my aging generation that will leave the earth in the not too distant future. Even now, there are fewer and fewer eyewitnesses still alive to reflect on the crucial personal stories of the previous century.

But a few of us who grew up in Stalin's Communist regime can still share their stories with the younger readers, and I am one of them.

My sincere appreciation to my dear friends Bruce and Patti Spencer, who enthusiastically volunteered to edit my manuscript, and who spent countless hours in fine-tuning it.

My friend and consultant Jeffrey Poelvoorde deserves my utmost appreciation for encouraging me to start writing this book and, together with David and Teresa Brigham, Dan and Elana Rappaport, became my first active and devoted listeners and readers.

Special thanks to Dr. Michael Ulm for his inspiration and great support during this endeavor of telling my story.

My son Jacob, who gave me the idea and the push to start writing some stories of my life and of the family history, mostly to share with the next generation of my grandchildren — thank you. I hope I exceeded your expectations.

And finally, to my husband Robert for being at my side through the whole process of reading and correcting my English language, reliving with me the roller coaster of my life with tears and sometimes laughter — thank you.

But most of all, I appreciate the blessed memory of my parents and all the rest of my heroes who gave me the voice to tell their stories.

Sergei, my Beloved, I am sure you are smiling...

INTRODUCTION

I remember how much I hated the required history classes in my high school in Leningrad — they were insufferably boring! All I was interested in was the day-to-day occurrences of my present existence and *to hell with the past*. I felt that we, young people, would change the world for the better anyway, and we really didn't have to know the past to live for the future.

Now, looking at the present from my pedestal of vast life experiences, I obviously feel differently. I now realize that I have lived and am living history! *Wow!!*

So the question for me is this: Is it possible to overcome the state of *human dementia* and somehow share these life lessons learned, so that young people can benefit from these valuable lessons of the past? I would like to make sure that the youth will never be lured into a false sense of security, oblivious to reality.

But how does the older generation present the lessons of history to a new generation to make them alive and interesting enough to read and accept as something of importance? How can we **all** learn the lessons of the past and understand their relevance to the present?

As I grow older, the story of my life is becoming more and more fascinating to me. The desire to share it with my family has also grown over the years, especially with the younger generation, and has caused me to contemplate some of the remarkable episodes of my past.

I have a valid skepticism as to whether anyone would have an interest at all in the things that happened to me and to our family over the past century. Yet, I find myself extremely eager to read anything about the history of my family. Unfortunately, my grandmothers and great grandmothers said not a word about their lives, so I have only unanswered questions about them. Perhaps they were illiterate or busy with their lives, perhaps they decided that nobody would ever be interested in their story, but then here I come along with my curious nature!

My fascination encourages me to overcome my doubts… and so I dedicate this effort to future generations who may be interested in the stories, adventures, misadventures, tragedies and miracles of my family.

Others outside of my family, however, may also find these events interesting and revealing. We were on the crossroads of history during the dramatic events of the twentieth century, experiencing and witnessing tyranny and oppression, persecution and deprivation on one side and great joy and blessings to raise our spirits on the other.

It may bring some enlightenment to those who seek to understand the dramatic happenings of the twentieth century, to know how these events affected everyday people such as my family and friends. It seems to me that the world has never learned much from history. With hope for a better future, we must never stop telling our stories.

This is my story…

PART ONE

THE SOVIET UNION

CHAPTER ONE

September 20, 2013. This date marks the fortieth anniversary of the most cataclysmic week in the life of the Okun family, consisting at the time of me, my husband Sergei and our 4-year-old daughter Anya.

The year was 1973. We were living in the city of Leningrad and after a year of waiting for permission to leave the Soviet Union, we finally received the key to our future, to our long-awaited freedom, to our new beginnings, and to unbelievable possibilities for us, our children and grandchildren.

A year previous, we had learned from Sergei's best friend Eizer that he had decided to apply for permission to leave Russia. To those of us living in the Soviet Union in the 1970s, this was a shocking, bold and risky move on his part. We were amazed by, and yet admired Eizer's decision, and it caused us to contemplate our own future. Sergei and I had never considered such a drastic move. But now, as we pondered a similar plan of action, our hearts were filled with fear, trepidation and excitement all at once.

We never expected that the doors of the prison that we lived in, called the Soviet Union, would ever be unlocked. For us it was like a life sentence to live in a country with no freedom, no dignity, and very few opportunities. In our loftiest dreams we would never believe that the communist system might ever allow any changes to occur. In our minds, as in the minds of real prisoners, we could only make the best of our given situation and create the best life possible under the circumstances.

We knew that life under the communist system was poverty-stricken, crippled, wretched, oppressive and bleak, but it was the only life we could ever have. We knew that as Jews we had an even more horrific atmosphere to deal with, considering endless anti-Semitism, persecution, and the prohibition of exploration of Jewish history or religion. Obviously, deep down in our souls we knew that we deserved better, but we tried not to let hopelessness and desperation overpower the youthful happiness of our day-to-day lives.

We never expected change, and we were not ready for change. We found ourselves dumbfounded and overwhelmed the minute Eizer told us his implausible news. The world of our uncomfortable but familiar prison cell was torn from underneath our feet and it turned our universe upside down.

Sergei and I couldn't sleep for weeks. We knew that if we attempted to leave the U.S.S.R., our life would never be the same. We knew right away that this would be the most important and difficult decision we would ever make. *To be or not to be…* To be free or to just exist, shriveling under the thumb of our repressive government. All it took was one of our friends who actually acted on the possibility of leaving the Soviet Union to allow us to imagine a similar path for us. The decision to leave crystallized very rapidly in our own minds.

To apply for permission to leave the Soviet Union meant to openly declare that we were now the Enemy of the Soviet People. We were betraying our country and committing treason. We were ready to leave Mother Russia, "the best country in the universe," and communism, "the best system in the world." And, being Jews, we would be treated like the most disgusting piece of trash. "The dirty Zionists want to go where? To Israel?? Insanity!!"

We understood that all the cards were on the table. If we should decide to do it, we would have to be ready to pay any price, knowing that the state had all the power to destroy us, to send us away, to take our daughter away from us and even to destroy our extended families. Nevertheless, we made our difficult decision. We didn't want to live the rest of our lives in a country with no freedom, under constant control of the state, in poverty and fear.

Sergei was the Moses of our Exodus. He was strong, uncompromising, and brave. He had been starving for the fresh air of freedom for a long, long time, going back to his childhood. He had grown up in the family of an Enemy of the People, while his father, Yakov, endured years in Stalin's labor camp prisons during the prime of his life.

We would have to announce our decision to our parents and siblings. Sergei was confident that his side of the family would accept that decision with enthusiasm. Not me...I was shaking, trembling, wondering endlessly what I should say to my parents and to my sister Lala and her husband, Mark. They had been married for about three years and their son Misha was just 2 years old. Mark had a huge extended family to which he was much attached and had a great job that he loved very much. Since he was preparing for the big day of his Ph.D. dissertation, we decided to wait and let him finish, before disclosing our alarming plans. We knew the rules of the game: if we had applied for emigration, Mark, as a family member, would not be given a chance to get his doctoral degree even if he himself had not applied for emigration.

In the meantime, my biggest worry and challenge was how to tell my mother and father. Which words would I use, and how would I explain that I was ready to leave them all behind with no real hope of ever seeing them again? If we were to immigrate to another country, Russia would not have let us return, even for just a brief visit. We were a very close family and my mother was not in good health. I was terrified that our decision would turn out to be a catastrophe for her and for all of us. My heart was very heavy, for I knew that my decision could break my mother's heart and separate our whole family forever.

I couldn't pray— I didn't know anything about God.
I couldn't tell my friends— everything was a secret from everybody.
I couldn't tell my sister.
I couldn't tell my little Anechka, whose life was depending on all those adult decisions...

It was just Me and my Beloved, whom I trusted and loved with all my might and all my heart. I believed in his vision to take us to the Promised Land. I was just twenty-seven years young, and was ready to go with him to the ends of the world.

CHAPTER TWO

After we had finalized our decision, we asked our friend Eizer, who was about to leave for Israel, to send us an official document, an affidavit, from an Israeli citizen with a request to the Soviet government for our emigration. That was the procedure that the government had established for all the Jews who wanted to leave the U.S.S.R. The only acceptable reason for letting us go was the reunification of separated families. The whole system was built on lies and deception. The official version of the reason for emigration was the humanitarian one, but we had no idea at that time how to make this happen, since we didn't know any relatives in Israel. And so one of Eizer's coworkers in Tel-Aviv became our fictitious relative, and kindly sent us all of the needed documents.

From this moment and until we actually got the fictitious invitation in the mail, we were "enemies in disguise" and our life continued under cover of normalcy. In reality, we were anxious, nervous, fearful, and overwhelmed.

I remember the day we came to announce our decision to the family. It was one of the happiest days of Mark's life, with a sense of unbelievable accomplishment and pride that we shared with him wholeheartedly. Mark's dissertation had been accepted, and he invited his family and friends to a party in celebration of his success.

By this time, we were at our wits' end and couldn't keep quiet for another day. After the party, it was time for us to shock our family.

It was the only time in my life that I was stuttering. Fortunately, Sergei was calm, collected and to the point. He simply told everybody that despite a great deal of emotional struggle and reservation on our part, we had decided to leave the U.S.S.R. for Israel.

It is impossible to imagine the complete chaos and disbelief in the minds of my parents, my sister Lala and Mark. It was like lightning and thunder in the middle of the absolutely blue summer sky. Their confusion and inability to understand and to comprehend the situation showed in the cacophony of the moment and extremely high emotions on everybody's part. There was the highest degree of discontent and misunderstanding, the feeling that we had lost our minds.

They pleaded with us to restore our sanity, to have mercy on my mother and in their anger, they accused us of insensitivity and selfishness. Fear prevailed: fear for everybody's future and fear of the unknown, fear of the neighbors, fear of what would happen to us and fear of what would happen to them, fear of the government and more fear and more fear...

And *why* would we want to destroy everything? We had good jobs, good apartments, a great city, family, friends, culture, and language. To exchange this all for what may prove to be illusions, when life is already good, when we are all together and Anechka and Misha love their grandparents and our bond is so strong, and we all have so much love for each other? And to go to Israel without any information or knowledge, without knowing the language? What if there will be no jobs and what if there will be no place to live and what if and what if and what if?

The next fear was for us to be so young and not truly understand the danger of this drastic request. They thought that it might prove to be a catastrophe for all of us. And they undoubtedly feared what might be the most painful agony to me: my mother would not survive all this tragedy.

I witnessed in horror my Mama's face — lost, distraught, panic-ridden, anxious and so, so sad...

But I don't remember tears — those came later. And I questioned myself. Was I strong enough to endure saying goodbye forever to my family? My poor, poor mother...

∞

For a few months, our everyday routine of life went on, although my heart was beating hard and my hands were shaking every time I opened our mailbox. We were not sure where we were headed, but we knew that we had already boarded the train and there was no way out. We knew that we could not turn away from the uncertain journey upon which we had set ourselves. The affidavit could come any day, and the clock was ticking.

Suddenly we felt like we were in a suspense movie, a horror movie, a movie with what could be a very bad ending. Before our drastic decision we were just regular invisible Soviet "happy citizens," never attracting any attention of the State to our existence, blending in with everybody else, remaining safely anonymous. That was soon to end.

I remember the day when we opened the mailbox and saw *THE ENVELOPE* with a strange foreign address and beautiful bright stamps. My first reaction was to look around to be sure that nobody saw it and no neighbors had witnessed its incriminating arrival. My body was shaking and my heart was ready to jump out of my chest. My head was spinning; it felt as if there was not enough air to breathe. We had been waiting for this day with trepidation and now it was *here!* I looked at little Anechka, who was holding Sergei's hand, smiling. I wish I would have been able to say some kind of prayer, but God's presence was unknown to me. I felt that for a few minutes time stopped and the awesomeness of the moment completely overwhelmed my consciousness. Life would never be the same, ever.

We had crossed the line, and now invisible radar was right over our heads. We had to be very careful, to know how to maneuver through all the legal procedures and preparations, to follow specific rules and regulations, to gather all the documents, papers, permissions, to satisfy even more regulations and requirements. But the first step was the most frightening of it all. We had to go to the government office with our affidavit and announce our decision to leave the U.S.S.R. and ask for their permission to do so.

That was the most terrifying day of my life. Until we opened the door of that office we still were "unannounced," but the second we entered the room we would be fully under their power and our future would be completely in their hands.

CHAPTER THREE

I remember sitting at the official table of the local deputy of foreign affairs. We saw the cold, expressionless, hard face of the woman who was assigned to our case. We felt small, insignificant, hopeless, and oppressed by the mighty power she represented. As she was reading our papers, the only sound in the silent room was the sound of our pounding hearts. We expected accusations and stern warnings, words of threat and actions against us, police-like warnings and more threats. But to our astonishment, when she started talking, her voice was calm and bureaucratic. She gave us instructions on how to take steps to prepare all the necessary papers and gave us a date to bring all the documents back to her. Sergei actually bravely asked her what would happen after the first round. She simply said that the decision about our future would be made at an indefinite time and we would be informed accordingly.

The next moment we were on the streets of our city Leningrad that I loved so much, where I grew up and had lived all my life. I looked around. Everything was the same and familiar, but everything was absolutely different. My perception of life had changed. Suddenly I had become a pariah. I had a secret and was concealing the real me. We were waiting for the "sentence" to be handed down, for harsh and unforgiving judgments and a trial without a jury. We knew that some invisible, unknown and indifferent bureaucrats would determine our future. Our lives were absolutely in the hands of those heartless people for whom we were just a case number. And all we wanted was to move from one place on this planet to another! Why was that such a treasonous crime? Why did the communist regime create such a prison behind the iron curtain? We had no political statements, no demands for any changes and no proclamations against the government. We just wanted to live in a different country.

In reality, we had no time for discussions, even with each other. Our limited time was consumed by following the myriad of instructions that had been given to us.

The first was the most troublesome one; we had to get a written character reference from our place of employment, which meant that we had to go to our respective bosses and reveal to them our plans. We feared — and our fears were realized — that this would simply provide the forum for all of our coworkers and the management to participate in a mandatory public ritual of accusing us of plotting Zionist and anti-Soviet activities.

I never was a part of any team at work. I was just a piano teacher, working diligently with a group of children. But I worked in the huge Cultural Center, which had many different departments. I really did not know any of the employees of the Center, but I was friendly with a few of the other piano teachers. However, the morning I announced my decision to my very Communist boss, I knew right away that everyone there would soon be very familiar with me as a symbol of dissenting and unacceptable behavior. My woman supervisor was the Director of the Children's Department and she barely knew me until that morning. I remember how horrified and pale she became after I disclosed my intentions to her. Her face changed immediately. Her eyes narrowed, her lips tightened and an expression of pure hate was immediately revealed. Her career, focused on the important job of raising little Communist children, was in jeopardy because of *me*. All through her professional life she had been on the front line of the Cultural Revolution. She had dedicated her life to promoting the ideas of socialistic art, and the idea of a "happy childhood" in the Soviet Union as the best childhood in the entire world. Her goal was to help to create art that praised the best system in the world in selected choices of music, children's plays, dances and songs. Every event was preplanned and preapproved, with no surprises. And now, my unexpected and sudden appearance in her office brought her to complete panic. Nobody could do this to her, especially not this despicable little insignificant Jewish Zionist piano teacher! *Nobody!*

Oh, I shall never forget her hateful face, ready to kill!! She couldn't hide her real poisonous feelings of disdain toward me, or her fear for her own career and future promotions on the communist party ladder. At first she did not know what to do, what to say, or how to react. This was unheard of! I was the first ever Zionist to make this request and on *her* watch? She needed instructions from above, consultations with her superiors and then she finally let me go.

After a week had passed, the announcement was made of a mandatory assembly of all the workers, which would be held after work hours. The agenda was to be the condemnation of my pending action and provocation taken against the great U.S.S.R. Finally, the day of the assembly arrived. Willingly or unwillingly, many people came, most of whom I had never seen before and who knew nothing about me. I was told to sit on the empty stage and listen to their speeches, without interruption or expression of my own thoughts. Sergei gave me some tranquilizer pills before I left home, knowing how vicious this assembly could become toward me. But even with this medication, something that I had never considered taking before, I was trembling. I am usually sensitive to emotional energy around me, and this event, charged with hostility, was the darkest and most negative I had experienced in my entire life.

One after another, they were screaming that I was a provocateur, a Zionist slave, a helper for aggression against Mother Russia, the enemy of their great country and their greatest ideas, an underground dissident, a Jewish zealot, and simply a sellout. They tried to outdo each other, their fists flying in the air, their faces red with rage, roaring, trying to slander and condemn me, trying to portray my future as a deservedly horrible failure of unbelievable proportions. They also ferociously declared Israel to be the worst Zionist cesspool of a country with its leaders and people as aggressors against humanity, warmongers, occupiers of lands of neighboring Arab countries and most of all, characterizing Israel as a rogue state which had no right to exist and which would not survive for more than a few years. One of the screamers predicted that my family and I would rot in hell and after Israel's fall, I would be begging Russia to let me back, but she would proudly refuse in revenge. There would be no forgiveness to a traitor who succumbs to the ideology of American Imperialism and Jewish Zionism.

I looked around. I knew they were instructed by the authorities to intimidate me. I also understood that this meeting had a larger purpose: terrorizing everyone else by setting me up as a public example who was forced to experience this hour of fear and trepidation, this hour of rejection by fellow citizens. My official tormentors surely hoped to scare the hell out of every other potential dreamer by demonstrating publicly the hard hand of the communist will and power. Overall, I believe that their show succeeded. I also presume that most of the speakers were absolutely sincere in their hatred for me as a Jew, and especially their hatred for Israel.

When I came home that night, I was extremely exhausted and spent, but I also felt relieved. This one part was behind me now and according to the instructions I would receive the needed papers the following week and be able to continue to work until the final determination of our fate was made.

Next it was Sergei's turn to go before the angry court of condemnation and to our big surprise, his request to his boss came at the same time as the requests of two other Jewish coworkers from his office. I don't know who was more alarmed, their boss or the three of them. In either case it didn't look good. It could have been seen as a group conspiracy, a Jewish underground group of some sort, a group of Engineer Zionists! Nothing could be treated more harshly than aspiring Jewish youth plotting some activities against the State. There were severe imprisonment sentences given for betrayal or support of the capitalistic ideology of America. Being sentenced as an enemy combatant could follow. Despite the fact that none of the possible accusations made any sense, were logical, or even applied to us, we were shaking in fear of the merciless outcome. The fabrication of anti-Soviet allegations was nothing new all during the era of building what was called the best system in the world. Prisons were overcrowded with so-called dissidents. We couldn't sleep in anticipation of the unknown consequences for us. Three friends, who would never disclose their plans to each other, were facing a trial from their coworkers and the administration.

But apparently the instructions from above were given to let them slide through and let higher authorities deal with the situation. So after a couple of weeks of real panic behind the scenes, all three of them were subjected to a public trashing similar to the one that I had undergone. It was a huge relief for all of us and for the future dreamers. Apparently, time was changing dramatically and we were paving the way for those who would come in the future. We were just bewildered for a long time as to *why* these events were occurring. What great forces were helping us all from outside of the prison that we had lived in for so long?

CHAPTER FOUR

We had about ten months of life between heaven and earth without any idea of what would be the final verdict for us. We knew that leaving the U.S.S.R. had been next to impossible for the last half century. People who applied for an exit visa were often persecuted, and sometimes imprisoned or placed in a psychiatric ward. *You must be insane to want to leave this paradise!!* We were completely isolated from the world. The government treated their citizens as animals in the zoo. They had all the keys and the power and they were keeping us under their full control. The ideologues of the U.S.S.R. successfully and tragically transformed the very nature of human beings. This was the system that brought out the absolute worst in people *by design*. We all felt like we were living in a prison without any way out.

The situation started to change after the victory of the Six-Day War in Israel in 1967. The atmosphere in the U.S.S.R. became even more terrible for Jews. They stigmatized us, always tried to make us feel inferior, and ridiculed and humiliated us. We had no official information about the Jewish State called Israel until suddenly all the newspapers were screaming about Israeli aggression against innocent Arab countries. This unexpected victory felt triumphant to us, despite the official negative narrative of the war. This event made a few of us brave enough to stand up against the Soviet regime and live in opposition to everything that we despised.

Time was moving very slowly. After all the papers and documents were given to the Office of Visas and Registration (OVIR), all the information and communication from the official quarter ceased and we lived in anticipation of the unknown. Anxiety was mixed with hope, tears with humor, fear with sadness, and silence with more fear. We shared our situation with only a couple of very close friends, whispering our thoughts and our plans. We didn't want to put anybody into jeopardy for being associated with pariahs.

Our family still was our main concern. What would happen to them if we would be allowed to leave, or not allowed to leave? What would happen to Anechka if they arrested us? If they will let us go, would our parents and siblings follow us, and if yes, what would happen to them? We had so many questions, but no answers for so long and really nobody to talk with or obtain information from. We tried to listen to *Voice of America*, but the authorities so successfully jammed the broadcast signal that we could barely hear anything.

What we really did not know that would have been very helpful to us to be aware of, was the international attention of people supporting the new wave of Jews who wanted to emigrate from the U.S.S.R. to Israel. After the unsuccessful act of hijacking a small airplane by a few unbelievably brave and strong young Jews in Leningrad, the story of their plea for freedom and demand for emigration was picked up by the foreign press and spread all over the U.S.A., Europe and Israel. The so-called hijackers were handed down harsh sentences at their trial, including a few death penalties, despite the fact, that *Operation Wedding* was stopped before the group even entered the airplane. And the purpose of the whole operation had simply been to bring the attention of the world to the desire of Jews to immigrate to their homeland. The results of the trial led to demonstrations and protests among Jews around the world. The demands of *"Let our people go!"* brought a shift and some changes in the U.S. policies toward Jewish emigration from the U.S.S.R. Two members of Congress, Senator Henry "Scoop" Jackson and Congressman Charles Vanik, believed that the Soviets had to be confronted, not appeased. I will always remember their names, because they put the Jewish emigration as a condition for the preferred status for the U.S.S.R. in the Trade Act. Their negotiations were successful. Russia needed grain for their starving citizens and so they simply sold Jews for *a loaf of bread* (at least, that was our perception of the events). That was actually the best solution for us. The only problem was that we had no idea about any of that during our long waiting period. Information was never available to us, as "animals in the zoo."

CHAPTER FIVE

The last chapter of our life in the U.S.S.R. is probably the hardest to write about. As I mentioned before, the waiting period was excruciating which had us walking on pins and needles for about a year. And then one ordinary and casual day in August 1973, the permission was given for us to leave! We were informed that we had only one month to get out!

Our disbelief, happiness, joy, excitement and hope were mixed with pain, tears and guilt. Until that day everything was unreal or surreal. We could hardly allow ourselves to dream about our future until this day, when even after a whole year of anticipation and preparation, it was a shocking and sudden realization — *This is it!!* Reality set in quickly. We had to follow the instructions and get ready in a very short time to leave everything and everyone behind, say goodbye and fly away into this elusive place called Israel.

Now everything started to speed up very rapidly and accelerate toward our day of exodus. We had no time for contemplating. Our main concern was to be sure to be prepared promptly and properly and to get all the new documents ready on time. Sergei had to fly to Moscow for some additional permission and visas, to get the tickets to fly to Israel through Vienna, figure out what was permissible to pack and send to Israel, and what was not.

It was also the right time to let all our relatives and friends hear our news, somehow without endangering their existence. We had to inform them one by one, not by the phone, but in public places. The reaction to this news from most of them was absolute shock and fear, incomprehension, and bewilderment. Most of them had never heard anything like this in their entire life. A few wanted to get more information, some were listening in awe and a very few caught the bug of the possibilities for themselves. We invited everybody to our farewell party with the full understanding that not many would come. Fear is often much stronger than all other emotions.

One month was barely enough time to finish all the preparations. The Soviet bureaucrats and their regulations were ruthless. Everything had to be on time and done according to their rules. We lived in fear of them and their power to reverse their decision to let us go. We were allowed to ship our furniture, some books and a few other things, but with a lot of restrictions. The list of things that we were allowed to take was very limited and it excluded any art collections, antiques, unique jewelry, ancient artifacts, rare books, certain musical instruments, pictures of the family members in Soviet uniform and just about anything of real value. I couldn't take my piano that I loved so very much, the best piano I could ever hope to have. They robbed us as much as they could. The day finally came, when everything was ready.

Meanwhile, the story of our impending departure was becoming a legend in certain circles among young Jews.

"The Okuns are leaving for Israel! Did you hear the unbelievable news? The Okuns are leaving for Israel!"

We were surprised to see many people whom we had never met before, attending our farewell party. They wanted to witness this event and to see this legendary couple. *Wow!* Some were begging us to take the addresses of their friends or relatives, or even giving us their addresses and asking us to send them an affidavit. Sergei was taking a risk by writing any information since it was not allowed by the State. Sadly, most of my relatives never showed up and I couldn't say my last goodbyes to them. Understandably, they had been paralyzed by fear. The gathering was at my parents' apartment and we were all whispering for fear that the neighbors would hear us and would take notice. We could never trust our neighbors, *never...*

All during this busy month we had no time to face our main source of pain, which was the separation from our families. Toward the end, it became somewhat easier, because my parents and Lala's family, after a lot of discussions and tribulations, decided to follow in our footsteps. A little hope began to develop in our hearts that maybe our separation would only be temporary!

Looking back, I wish I would have had the slightest idea about the existence of God and His mighty power, understanding and trusting that God was watching over us and helping our family all along the way, but I didn't have any knowledge of God then, or for a long time after. Faith in God and prayers would have been so helpful, if I had only known.

Nothing helped me on the day of departure. As I was hugging my sister, my mother and father, I felt that I would never see them again, as long as I lived. How can I describe the sorrowful and tragic scene at our departure? I was holding my Mama; the tears were flowing down. My Mama was barely holding herself together. I was trying to comfort her with some words of hope. "This is not the end, Mama, it is just a beginning. We will see each other again. I love you Mama and Papa, thank you for being such wonderful parents to me. Thank you for all your help and love...and please, please, take care of yourselves! I want you to be healthy, because I want to see you in Israel."

I wanted to freeze this moment in time, to preserve this moment, to prolong this terrible moment, to scream that I didn't want to say *goodbye forever...* I didn't want to leave my Mama and Papa behind! I wished that these hugs and kisses would never end and would last forever. I looked at my sister, my only sister with whom I am so close. Would I ever see her again? I was leaving my parents in her care, not knowing what might happen to them after we left.

"Lalechka, my dear, I broke the covenant of the family and I am leaving my parents and you behind. Will I ever see you and your little son Mishenka again?" Everybody was hugging and kissing little Anechka, who was about to board the airplane for her first flight, her first venture away from home. Sergei, trying to keep his emotions under control, finally took me gently by my hand and led me out of the building toward the airplane. Finally... *It's time!*

I looked back and for the last time saw my family waving goodbye, everybody trying to smile through their tears. My poor, loving Mama!

After experiencing so much pain in her life she was forced to stand there and experience the anguish of saying goodbye for the last time to her first-born daughter.

As I was boarding the plane, my tears, which I tried to suppress earlier for my parents' sake, poured out like a flooded stream. I was holding Anechka's hand. She looked up, perplexed, and asked me why I was crying. She was so excited to get onto the plane and fly! She was my little angel as we walked to the airplane and I tried to remind myself that her future was one of my primary reasons for leaving our old life behind.

Then came one of the most exhilarating, elating, thrilling, unforgettable, one-of-a-kind moments of my entire life. As the plane took off and I was holding Sergei's hand, my tears of sadness and despair suddenly started to turn into breathtaking tears of unbelievable happiness and joy!

We are flying to freedom!   We just left the worst country in the world behind!

WE... ARE...FREE!!!

Chapter Six

Before leaving Russia for Israel, I had never flown on an airplane. Flying was far too expensive for ordinary citizens. We always traveled by train and spent a few days getting to our destination, which was mostly going to the Black Sea for summer vacation. But flying abroad? This was an unheard-of privilege that few Soviet people ever experienced. Flying was reserved only for the privileged few: Communist Party heads, big shots, sport teams, some great performers or scientists. They had to have a special permission from the officials of the State to fly abroad, but only under the watchful, probing eyes of Communist supervisors.

Nobody was allowed to escape, to talk with anyone, or to walk away from the group without permission from above. No one would dare to defect, but we heard rumors that a few brave ones did, such as the famous ballet dancers Rudolf Nureyev and Natalia Makarova. It was a scary sensation for all of us, especially after the outpour of condemnation for those traitors by the Soviet press and the public opinion of the Soviet working class.

We, the few Jewish families allowed to immigrate, were an unlikely group. It seemed to us, strangely enough, that nobody on the plane was watching us! The memory of this most difficult month of our lives is still vivid — the cruelty of the border security agents, torturing us and treating us like criminals, as they were checking every object of our meager baggage. We knew that if they found anything that they deemed inappropriate, they could prevent us from leaving. There was an inspection a week before our departure, when we were sending our big items such as furniture by sea, and once again before boarding the plane. We were so nervous, with our knees shaking and our hearts beating out of our chests, even though in reality, we were so poor that we could not imagine what in the world they hoped to find. Diamonds? Unfortunately, we could see the delight in their faces in demeaning these insignificant Jews. Hate was in the air, and maybe jealousy, too.

The truth is that we didn't even comprehend how very, very poor we were. That came later, and the realization was shocking. The rule was that we could exchange our rubles for a maximum of $120 per person, and the rest of our hard-earned money stayed in Russia. They tried to make things as difficult for us as possible, but for reason unknown to us and to our surprise, by the end of the day, they had to show us the door and tell us, "Get out of here!" (Again, that was the instruction from above, which I mentioned before). Upon boarding the plane, however, we suddenly became the "privileged class," and surprisingly, the stewardesses treated us almost like the rest of the passengers. It was the first time in our lives that we had experienced a measure of courtesy instead of insolence. It was unbelievable to us.

We had to stop and change planes in Poland. A couple of other Jewish families were traveling with us, and we were happy to meet them. As we were looking around in amazement at the different environment in the Polish airport, I remember that one of the women came back from the restroom, and with wide open eyes and an expression of delight, told us to go and to check it out. "It's amazing, amazing!"

I took Anechka with me and was as surprised as the other woman. I remember that it was my second *wow* in just a couple of hours. I probably never had seen a "normal" clean public restroom before, though it is hard for me now to relate to this girl and her discovery of the world, even knowing that it was ME. I just know that for whatever reason, this episode got stuck in my head. Russia was a very dirty place in all aspects of human life. And it was already far behind us physically, but so far only physically.

We landed in Vienna late in the evening absolutely exhausted, especially Anechka. Some agent was waiting for us there and directed us to the bus. *Wow!* What a great bus it was! They told us that we were going to the Shenau Castle near Vienna with an escort of a couple of police cars, since times were very dangerous. That was a precaution against terrorists. What terrorists? Who were the terrorists and why? We had no idea what they were talking about, but at this point we just wanted to get to some place for a good rest. After all, it was still the same day that we started in the morning at my parents' apartment after our goodbye party.

The bus was moving so smoothly, and the view from out of the window was like a foreign movie that we had never seen and only imagined. It was a different world on this planet: different energy, different landscape, different people, and different air, different everything. We were passing some streets on the outskirts of Vienna, but still, it looked so foreign — bright lights, fluorescent advertising, enchanting windows of the beautiful stores and so many cars. *Wow!* But poor Anechka was absolutely overtired and exhausted. She started to throw up all over herself. I guess that's life. Children can bring you to reality very quickly. In any case, we got to this fairytale-like castle at nighttime and went straight to bed.

The morning was glorious. We woke up in a gorgeous castle with breathtaking grounds that we thought existed only in the movies. Breakfast was fit for a king, and there were polite people around us. Was I dreaming? *Wow!*

We were in this castle for a few days — resting, relaxing, and enjoying talking with people without looking around and behind us. There was nobody to be afraid of, nobody was abusing us, and nobody was telling us what to do! *Wow!* But we were very uncertain and naïve. We did not really comprehend what was going on around us, did not know what to do, what to think, where to go.

One of the single guys suggested to us, "I am going to Vienna. Who wants to go with me?" What? How could we just decide to go anywhere without permission from some authority? Who would we ask? Who can tell us the rules? "No, no we can't!" was our answer. We didn't want to overstep our boundaries. We were raised like animals in the zoo and we got used to being behind the gate. Even when the gate was open, we couldn't step out. We were *free*, but we had no idea what freedom really meant.

We didn't realize at that moment that we had the best status on the world scene — the status of *Refugee from the U.S.S.R.*, a status that gave us freedom to choose any country we wanted to emigrate to — U.S.A., Canada, Australia, New Zealand, France, etc. We did not ask questions, did not talk with anybody about our rights as refugees, or what our possibilities were. We were following the orders and instructions of our Soviet bosses like good Soviet sheep. All we were told was that the Soviet emigration agency gave us visas to leave the U.S.S.R. for Israel.

There were some young Israeli agents in the castle, and they asked us a few questions and told us to fill out some applications. They were happy to see us and welcomed us with smiles and enthusiasm. And then they told us, that since we had agreed to go to Israel, we would be leaving tomorrow. *Agree to go to Israel?* What a strange statement it was for us to hear. What would have happened if we had disagreed? Did we have a choice? The answer was "Yes," but we didn't even know enough to ask.

It took us a long time to begin to understand what was happening to us and around us in the Shenau. Some people had more information than we had, but very few requested visas to other countries, including the U.S.A. I don't know what our decision would have been if we had been more informed. Maybe our life would have gone in a completely different direction. That might have been possible, but considering our Soviet-induced state of unawareness and fear, the decision was made for us, not by us.

The morning flight to Israel was delightful. This was the first time we had seen young Israelis, who were on our flight returning to Israel. They looked absolutely stunning, wearing beautiful clothes, speaking a strange Hebrew language and had many young children around. Happy faces, an atmosphere of high energy, enchantment, joy, a different breed of people that we never had seen before... *Wow! Wow! Wow!* On our landing approach, I remember looking out the window and, for the first time seeing the Promised Land, excitement overwhelmed me... *Wow! Wow! Wow!*

I can't explain the euphoria that I felt at that moment. There is something so special for Jews, when they come to the Holy Land. I looked at Sergei and, for the first time, saw him very emotional, almost crying.

The excitement was even stronger when we touched the ground and everybody started clapping, singing and hugging.... *Wow! Wow! Wow!*

What a long journey we had been through to come to this point. Israel is not an Illusion. It is a real land, a real beautiful country, with real people and all of them were Jews! Real songs, a real airport, and then finally, our friend Eizer, standing behind the glass, smiling and waving his hands.

"Shalom! Welcome home, Okuns!"

PART TWO

ISRAEL

CHAPTER SEVEN

Israel — one of the strongest memories of my life…
The end of September 1973 was the beginning of a new chapter of our life. We were in a different space in the universe, with diverse and unexpected dynamics, discovering slowly a life without fear, oppression, darkness, and submission to the power of others. Emigration is a very complicated and unpredictable process for everyone, but for us, it was, at first, an act of dislocation, relocation, and disorientation. Since we had no information about our new homeland, in my imagination, I was going to Paris or something close to it.

Driving with Eizer (in his own car — *Wow!)* to our destination in Haifa was more than fascinating. *This is nothing like Paris,* I was thinking. Surprise, surprise! We were in a Middle Eastern country, with much more Arabic landscape and natural surroundings than I ever could have imagined. I was holding Sergei's hand tighter, looking around with excitement, disbelief, and also with some disappointment.

Israel was beautiful, but it was different than I had envisioned. The ocean reminded me of the Black Sea that we loved so much, and the weather was warm, breezy, and summerlike for us northerners who, just a few days prior to this moment, were preparing for the harsh, cold winter in Russia. It seemed to us that we had come for a vacation in this foreign land. Eizer was sharing a lot of information, giving us some instructions, explaining some necessary rules, trying to bring us up-to-date. I barely could keep my attention focused; so much chaos was in my head. Anechka was sleeping calmly, and looking at her angelic face, I was nervously opening myself up to a new life in this new, untested country.

Eizer drove us to the Absorption Center, or *ulpan;* the place where emigrants could live and study Hebrew for about four months, before starting life on their own. The *ulpan* in Haifa was occupying the old whorehouse, used by men during the English Mandate times. *"Bruchim Habaim — Welcome Home,"* exclaimed the smiling faces in the office. We got a small room on the second floor, brought in our luggage, and Eizer, after many hugs and kisses, left for his home in Tel-Aviv. He invited us for Rosh Hashanah in a couple of days. "It is the High Holiday season," he tried to explain, but we had no idea what he was talking about. We had never heard those words before — *Rosh Hashanah, Yom Kippur?*

Our diaspora had lasted too long. As Russian Jews we were estranged and alienated from the history, tradition and any knowledge of religion, especially Judaism. The concept of God was laughable, primitive, and only for uneducated people. We were superior to this nonsense. Before the revolution in Russia and over the centuries for Jews all over the world, there was a longing, passion and hope to immigrate to the Holy Land. Not for us. We were absolutely assimilated secular Russian Jews and extremely oblivious of Jewish beliefs or customs; even more so than some other Russian Jews in Leningrad, and especially those who came from the southern parts of the U.S.S.R..

I remember our first train trip to see Eizer and his family: young soldiers with guns over their shoulders filled the train, going home for the holidays. We were amazed by the scene. Why were there so many soldiers? We had never seen anything like this before. Very young men and women? Why? Where were they all going? They were all a little younger than us- why were they all in uniform? How come they look so happy and not disturbed? They looked so handsome; I was thinking, *Wow, Jewish boys are so good-looking!* But many of them looked so, so different from our stereotype of the weakly Russian Jews. They all looked so strong and physically trained. Girls are soldiers too? Why? Beautiful, tall, suntanned, and looking so exotic, with guns? What is going on?

Eizer explained to us a little bit of what was happening, but many questions were not answered. We had so many other things to discuss. Also, since it was a peaceful time between the Six-Day War and the Yom Kippur War, we had not talked about politics yet. We just did not know that we had only a few days of peace left.

CHAPTER EIGHT

We were surprised and delighted to learn that relatives from France had come to Israel to welcome us. Sergei's Uncle Yanek (his mother's brother) and Yanek's wife Simone flew especially to greet us in our new homeland. It was a very happy occasion, since those families had been separated from each other since 1932 until now, and Sergei was meeting them for the very first time. Communication was difficult, since they didn't know Russian. Sergei brushed up on his French as best he could.

Yanek and Simone introduced us to the "good life." They drove us around to show us the beauty of Haifa — the shoreline, the warm beaches, Mount Carmel, the Baha'i World Center with its golden-domed shrine and breathtaking surrounding gardens. The following day, Yanek and Simone wanted to surprise us with some gifts and took us to downtown Haifa into expensive stores to buy some clothes and sandals for summer. Our own clothes were so worn and old-looking, not only to us, but especially to these fashionable Parisians! As we were window-shopping, I could hardly believe my eyes: gorgeous dresses and shoes that were colorful, fashionable, and there were so many choices! Unlike in Russia, there were no lines of people waiting patiently for their turn to buy — shocking! The sales ladies were smiling, polite, and ready to help us. I felt in Seventh Heaven again, like I was in a foreign movie! In this new colorful outfit and in new platform sandals, I felt like a movie star! Am I? And Anechka was looking like a doll, so pretty and happy.

Simone introduced us to her family who lived in Haifa; her cousin Ada and her husband Shmerl. Both were Holocaust survivors. Eventually, Ada and Shmerl became very close friends of ours. We were invited to Ada and Shmerl's home for a delightful and heartwarming dinner — our first family dinner abroad! After dessert they told us that the next day would be the Jewish holiday of Yom Kippur, the Day of Atonement, which meant that most everyone in the entire country would go to the synagogue. All the stores and businesses would be closed, and no cars would drive on the street. It is a day of repentance, a quiet day for God. We had no idea what they were talking about. What was this story? What God? We were just excited to go to Yanek and Simone's hotel the following morning and spend a quiet day there.

Israel seemed to be a peaceful and happy place, and we loved being with our family. We were starting to think more positively. Our *ulpan* orientation will start after the Holy Days, and then we will start building our new life. We also planned to send an affidavit for an emigration request to my sister and my parents. When they would come to Israel, we would all live happily ever after. Sergei and I were both genuinely happy for the first time in a long, long time. We will adjust and integrate into this country. Thank you, Simone and Yanek — you helped us to cross the bridge, and tomorrow, we'll have a nice Yom Kippur together.

The morning was unusually quiet when we walked to the hotel to meet the family on October 2, 1973. Not only we, as new emigrants, but the whole country had no idea what was coming next.

I was looking out of the window of the hotel and marveled at the serenity of the streets, exactly as Uncle Yanek told us. There were no people, no cars, no movement. It was a moment of tranquility, peacefulness, and striking stillness. There was an almost unreal calmness in the air...

Then suddenly, at about two o'clock in the afternoon, everything started to change. I saw the first moving car, then another and more. Young soldiers were jumping into the cars with all their guns and ammunition. Across the street, women and children were coming outside, kissing and hugging their men-soldiers as they were driving away in their cars, waving goodbye, blowing kisses; no crying, though.

What kind of bluff is this, I wondered. *As strange as it is, not everybody is following the rules of Yom Kippur.* I called to Sergei, who was talking with his uncle and holding Anya on his lap, to show him my discovery out of the window.

"What have they been telling us? It is not true! The cars didn't move only in the morning, why? Do you understand why? What is going on?"

I saw Shmerl and Uncle Yanek listening to the radio.

"But they told us that listening to the radio is not allowed on Yom Kippur!"

What's happening? Uncle Yanek's and Shmerl's faces were getting darker, worried, and more stressed. They listened to the horrible news and did not know what to tell us or how to explain what they themselves could barely understand.

It is a WAR, an unexpected war, and an unprepared-for war. Oh, my God, I thought, A W-A-R, like a real war?? With whom? Who is the enemy? Why?? Why?? What should we do?? Where should we go?? Where can we hide? How to hide our Anechka? Oh, my God – My poor Mama, my poor family in far-away Russia! They told me not to go, not to break up the family, and now… My father, a World War II veteran who almost lost his life twice, being gravely wounded, and survived only by a miracle; what is he thinking now, how is he dealing with my mother? She is probably losing her mind!

After a while, Uncle Yanek told us that he had called the airline to change their tickets, and that they would be going back to Paris the next morning. But what about us? We don't know what to do with ourselves. We want to go to Paris, too! We do not have anybody here, and we don't know anybody. We are lost, lost, lost…

At night, back in our room, looking at our daughter sleeping, we felt even more lost. And then suddenly, through the stillness of this night, in the quiet of the darkness, we heard for the first time in our lives, the thundering sound of the *Hazaka* — the air raid siren — that we knew only from the war movies that we had seen in Russia. We heard people running downstairs, children screaming. Sergei grabbed sleeping Anechka and told me to run after him to the special underground shelter.

When we entered the place, we saw a lot of newcomers who had arrived at the *ulpan* during the last week from Russia and Romania to start a new life. Women of the older generation were sobbing, crying, screaming something in Yiddish. For them, it was all déjà vu. They thought they were back in the horrifying times of World War II. Children were crying, because they were awakened in the middle of the night and saw their distraught parents acting like they had never seen them act before. I was holding Anechka, thinking that this was supposed to be a glorious time for us to enjoy the beginning of our new life, and now what?

CHAPTER NINE

All through my life, I had felt and seen so much *hate*, *hate* and more *hate*. It started from the very early years of my life. Those times were extremely tough for people around me, growing up in postwar Russia. Being a child, I had yet to understand what was happening in my small world, beyond my loving family.

My first memories are of the unconditional love of my grandma, Babushka Meita. What a God-given blessing for a little girl, born into a world of hate. Babushka passed away when I was only 7 years old, more than half a century ago, but she has remained with me throughout my entire life. She spoke some Russian, but mostly Yiddish, unlike all the people around me.

"Why, Babushka, do you say funny words?" I would ask as a young child. Her response was,

"We are Jews, and that is our language. Other people are Russians, so they speak the Russian language."

This was alarming and unsettling to me. I did not want to be different; I wanted to be like everybody else. I thought that since I did not look different, maybe others would not know that I am Jewish, whatever that means. But her love, warmth, kindness and caring softness toward me would calm down my worrying mind. I barely remember, but I heard her talking to "Gottele" or something like this, maybe praying, but she never explained to me, who she was conversing with at night.

From the start, I felt the contrast between the safe world with my grandma and my parents (whom I saw very little, since they were at work six days a week), and the world surrounding us.

We lived in the smallest place on the first floor in back of a big building with a lot of communal apartments, where people shared one room per family of four, five or even more people. Each apartment had five to ten

or more rooms with one communal bathroom, no shower, and one kitchen
for all the women to share. The conditions were inhumane by all accounts.
But my parents happened to have their small separate apartment, without
roommates. It was better situation for us and made my sister and I feel
very special. Our home was this tiny, dark, humid hole-in-a-wall place with
no daylight, full of mold, with wallpaper falling off the walls from the
humidity. The tiny kitchen was without a window and had one small kerosene stove for my grandma to cook dinners for six people.

Living in this condition, and breathing mold all year long, contributed
to our frequent sickness during our childhood. It was especially hard on my
Mama. But this place was ours alone. It had been a horse stable before my
parents got permission, after they were married, to transform it into some
kind of livable dwelling. The fact that Jews were living in a separate apartment caused resentment among our neighbors. The only other separate
apartment near ours was occupied by the family of a KGB agent.

This neighborhood provided my first encounter with *hate*. Babushka
would let me go to play outside, and the neighbor's kids would scream
"*Jidovka* (a derogatory name for a Jew), go home. We don't want to play
with you." And even after a while, when they would get used to me and see
that I was a sweet girl, they still had no other name for me, but *Jidovka*. I
felt like an outsider, disliked. I felt their desire to hurt me, to bully me, but
why? "*Jidovka, Jidovka, Jidovka…*"

There was another aspect of *hate* that I experienced at the same time.
It seemed to me that all our neighbors hated each other, too. We were
surrounded by working people who were trying to rebuild their lives after
the war. Men came back wounded, disturbed, beaten down, and hungry.
Living conditions were horrific. Money was scarce, and there was not
enough to support a family. Cold, brutal winters, overcrowded public
transportation — it was a nightmare for everybody. Post-traumatic stress
disorders were usually self-treated by large quantities of vodka. There was
plenty of domestic violence in the families between husbands and wives,
children and fathers. There were loud disputes between members of families. How did I know? I heard women screaming and children crying, men

swearing, as they were beating their wives and sons from behind the walls. Especially on the days of receiving their minuscule salaries, vodka was contributing to the violence, and the walls were shaking.

I wanted to disappear, to fly away, to hide, and just not to hear this human despair. Even today, it is hard for me to hear people screaming and being violent toward each other. My family seemed to me like they came from another planet.

"Why are we here?"

Babushka would try to hug and kiss me and console me saying,

"Goyim like vodka too much, more than they love their families. Jews are different. We love each other more and we do not subscribe to violence."

The worst time in my childhood came after my grandmother's sudden death at the age of 63. My world stopped. I lost the soul closest to me, a pure love that has carried me, I think, all through my life. In the hardest moments of my life, I remember her. She is my angel, watching over me, protecting me, guiding me, and always waiting for me... I had just turned seven years old when she left us. I hardly really remember her at all. It is our spiritual connection that I treasure.

But after Babushka died, my earthly safe world was over. Because of our violent neighbors, I would be afraid to be home alone after school until my mother would come from work and bring my little sister from the kindergarten. So I would stay outside, where people were walking about, and wait, wait, and wait, even in the windy, unbearable winter weather. *Hate* would show its ugly face time and time again. Drunken men would be walking, barely standing on their feet, zigzagging, falling and getting up and singing the Russian drunken song, *'Shumel kamish, derevya gnulis!'* and screaming with all their might,

"Kill the Jews and save our Mother Russia." Or even more profound,

"Let's finish the job that Hitler did not finish."

I wanted to become invisible, to stop breathing, to stop shaking. I had a nauseating, crippling fear that they were coming after me, who else? There were no other Jews around, just me, only ME… Why do they hate me so much, what did I do to them and who are these *Jews* that I am suffering for? Babushka told me that we *are* good people, that my father never hurt anyone. He fought in the Red Army of the Soviet Union in War World II and was wounded twice, and he had many medals for bravery that I loved to look at with fascination.   My poor mother had lived through the horrible starvation during the blockade of Leningrad. So why did they hate me? Why? The only salvation that I had was that it was dark on the streets, so they just could not find me this time. Maybe tomorrow would be a better day. *Mama, I am waiting for you to come and save me, why are you so late?* After a long time I finally would see my mother and my sister, whom I adored; now I would be safe for tonight. I didn't want to tell Mama the truth about why I was waiting outside, instead of being home and practicing my piano.

Things only got worse. The last years of Stalin's life were deadly for Jews of the U.S.S.R. Out of pure hate, Stalin wanted to inflict as much pain as possible, just short of finishing Hitler's job of extermination by killing us all. I knew that something bad was going to happen very soon. It was in the air, in my parent's faces, in my school. The teacher asked all the Jewish kids to stand up and show their faces to everybody. I knew that I must get up and could not just hide under the desk. With trembling legs, I stood up and to my surprise, one other student stood up behind me. I thought, *What are they going to do to us now? Kill us, beat us up?*

I loved my teacher. I was an excellent student, and I thought the teacher loved me. *What did I do wrong? Why is it so bad to be Jewish?* The whole class looked at me with child-like hate, not from inside, but learned from the adults. The other kids were my friends until that day. The fact that I was a Jew hadn't come up yet. I had hoped it never would. I did not look or act differently, except at the beginning of the school year, I was pronouncing the letter *R* like my grandma and Mama, more like the French *R* than Spanish, and I heard myself sound differently, but Mama had helped me through the speech therapist to correct it a long time before this day.

A life of hate toward me continued long after Stalin's death. In summers, my parents would send my sister and me to the Young Pioneer Camp for a *"good and joyful time."* I didn't want to go, but I had no choice. My parents were working and nobody could watch my sister and me. My memory is mixed. For the first couple of weeks, everything would go smoothly — I would make friends, participate in all the activities, sing songs, and pretend that I was enjoying it, especially in my letters home. Then, the camp would have a parent's visiting day, and by the time they would leave the camp, I would feel the drastic change. Nobody would know that I was a Jewish kid because I didn't look Jewish. My parents, on the other hand, looked like real Jews. So at night, a group of inquisitors would come close to me and, hiding their fists, would ask me if it was true, that they had discovered my real identity. I wonder sometimes, if they would have left me alone, if I would have lied. The remaining part of the summer would be full of hate toward me, bullying and beating me up every time when the counselors were not around. I never cried, I just was asking them *"Why?"* What did I do to them?

When I became older I still had more questions than answers. My parents would preach to me, "Always be proud to be Jewish. Jews are good, intelligent, talented people, hardworking, and they do not drink. They like to study. When you grow up, only marry a Jewish man — we have to continue the Jewish heritage. They are very good husbands. Also, many very talented and famous people are Jews." I would just shake my head in disbelief, thinking that, with all due respect, my parents, especially Mama (since she would try her hardest to reinforce these ideas), just didn't understand anything. *To be proud? For all those lame reasons? To live in fear for what? To be hated?* I had to find better answers, the *truth*, andb etter explanations.

I didn't know any Jewish girls all through my school years, and only a few Jewish boys from my class. I would ask my Russian girlfriends,

"Why do they hate the Jews, but would be good friends with me?" Their answer:

"You are different. We like you, because you are not like all of them."

"But do you know any other Jews, because even I can't find one? Apparently they are all spread around, and except for my extended family, I have never met any of them." The answer was,

"No, we don't know any other Jews, but we hate them anyway."

We were all atheists; God didn't exist for any of us. But it didn't change the hate, though sometimes they would confess to me, whispering,

"Those dirty Jews, besides all their other crimes, killed our Iisus Christos — Jesus Christ!!"

I myself didn't like, that Jews killed this Russian guy with such a strange name. *How did they know that it happened? Who told them? Why did Jews kill him? Was he a bad guy? But what does this have to do with me?* I heard that some of their grandmothers and even their parents were referring to this strange name from time to time. But for some reason they blamed *me* for being part of some conspiracy from long ago? *Why did they beat me up for this?* I had so many unanswered questions in my early childhood, and unfortunately, I still do.

CHAPTER TEN

I did not have any Jewish friends until I was accepted into the Music College in Leningrad. That was a new and optimistic discovery. I was not alone, and there were other Jews besides me and my extended family. But the *Simchat-Torah* celebration of 1968 changed me and the direction of our family history forever.

Sergei and I were married by that time, and we lived our quiet happy life of bliss and adoration of each other. The Jewish identity was not on our agenda, but I was content to be able to fulfill my parents' request to marry a Jewish man and, maybe in the future, to have a Jewish child. To me, it was much more important that I married my real soul mate, a wonderful person, my Beloved. His Jewishness was only a plus.

On an autumn day in October 1968, things started to change, to shift. I got a telephone call from my cousin Alik that there was a celebration of the Jewish Holiday in the synagogue. "Come, Ella, and bring your sister with you. It will be a great event. Come, you'll be thrilled," exclaimed Alik enthusiastically.

What Holy Day? What is Simchat-Torah? What does it mean? To go to the synagogue? Isn't it dangerous? Where is the synagogue? Actually, it was just around the corner from my college, but I had no idea and no interest to know. The synagogue, in my mind, was only for some really old people, like sixty years old, older even than my parents, still in their fifties.

Some families were much closer to Jewish traditions than my own and kept all that under "deep cover" in their homes. A few of the older people were even going to the synagogue! It was a dangerous place for the younger generation to simply peek in and show their faces. Even without the surveillance cameras back then, the KGB would know who we are!

∞

My cousin Alik shared with me many stories of our extended families, some of which were unknown to me until recently. Alik came from the family of my father's favorite cousin Meyer. As unbelievable as it sounds, my Uncle Meyer or Misha (his new Russian name), was not only instrumental in introducing my parents to each other at one of his parties, but also in my introduction to my beloved Sergei many years later. Alik's grandpa Simon was born in 1879 and his sister, my grandma Malka, was born in 1887. They were children of Aaron Korobochko who had three sons and only one daughter. They grew up in Belorussia in a very religious traditional Jewish family. In the early years of the twentieth century, when many Jews were leaving Russia for America, all three brothers somehow decided to leave for South Africa to seek a better life. Simon probably got engaged before the trip and, following his heart, came back to fulfill his obligation. He married Freida-Rohel and for some reason, unfortunately, they never went back to South Africa. They had 13 children. All but five died when they were young children. What a horrible burden for the parents to carry through their entire life!

After the revolution, when the Bolsheviks came to power, they started the shakedown. They wanted to confiscate all possible gold from the 'wealthy' Jewish families. Simon and Freida-Rohel owned a small boarding house and were considered to be rich Jews, so the Bolsheviks arrested Freida-Rohel and demanded gold. She refused and told them that she had none. Interrogating and forcing her to walk barefooted in the snow with no winter jacket didn't change her attitude. She still insisted she had none (though, she told Alik many years later that she had hidden some). Finally, they let her go home for the night.

By the next morning, the family had chosen to flee away from the dangerous pogrom zone. The quick decision was made by Freida–Rohel, who was much more decisive than her husband. She told her son Meyer, then 15 years old, to stay behind to sell their house and the cow, which he did before joining the rest of the family in the place of escape. Freida-Rohel's next plan for Meyer was to leave Belorussia and to go to Stalingrad, where there were more chances to find a better job. She promised him that the family would join him in a while, after he established himself in a big city. A person in front of Meyer at the railway ticket window asked for a ticket to Leningrad, and since the names of both cities sounded the same to him, Meyer asked for a ticket to the same place as the man before him. And so this little mistake enabled our whole family, including our Guretzky clan, to escape to the best city in the Soviet Union, called Leningrad. An unbelievably fortunate break of a lifetime!!

In the late 1920's, Meyer's family had to escape from their shtetl once again. This was deeply devastating to them, but most of their relatives who stayed in Belorussia were eventually murdered by the Nazis during the occupation of Belorussia. We never know when something seemingly tragic happens to us, that in the long run, our apparent misfortunes can be a blessing in disguise. My father Isaac also followed his favorite cousin-Meyer to Leningrad in the late 1920's. What a great decision that was for my family.

In Leningrad, Simon continued being a pious Jew all throughout his life despite the danger under Communist rules, prohibitions and prosecution. He created a small underground world where he would spend most of his free time reading the Talmud, studying Torah, and praying. Simon was a brilliant, educated scholar — a brave, but quiet man. He always wore *tzitzes* (religious undergarment) and had a *shofar* (rams horn) at home for celebration of the Jewish High Holidays. Nothing and no one would stop Simon and his wife from celebrating Jewish holidays, praying and even having Passover Seder with homemade *matzos* (unleavened bread) on the table. They kept a kosher home and Simon even insisted that all the newborn boys in his family would have a *Bris* (circumcision) according to the Jewish law, performed by the lay *mohel*, since there were no professional *mohels* around and the whole procedure was prohibited under Soviet law. Some people are just born fearless no matter what, and even though Simon's family was forced to keep the Jewish tradition hush-hush from the world around, they did not let it die.

I always was fascinated by my cousin's family and met Freida-Rohel a few times, after she became a widow. She impressed me as being very strong-willed, uncompromising, and had a fearless Jewish spirit. She was also a very beautiful old lady, and I can only imagine her beauty in her youth! No wonder Simon came back from faraway South Africa to marry her. The whole family consisted of exceptionally beautiful people. But Alik's older sister Vera was probably the most gorgeous girl in the whole city of Leningrad; at least I thought so. She looked to me very much like a young Freida-Rohel, a quintessential Jewish beauty with a mysterious light shining through her dark eyes. Despite all her adversities and hardships, Freida-Rohel had a long life and never lost her cleverness and wit. She passed away at age 98 —the oldest person I ever knew personally.

Unfortunately, our families were not close at all. It is painful for me to look back and understand how much I missed growing up without being close to the Korobochko family. Their children had a completely different upbringing than Malka's grandchildren. I wish I would have known Dedushka Simon and Babushka Freida-Rohel more intimately, had more exposure to their inner world and had some understanding of their Jewish identity. The pity is that the division of the families occurred over some nonsensical dispute between the older generations many years prior to the time that I came around. Later in life I understood that it was not a very unusual situation among Jewish families — typical, but very sad.

Nevertheless, I am forever grateful to Alik for the connection that we always had and still have. And in some way his telephone call for the Rosh-Hashanah celebration in the fall of 1968 became a turning point in our lives.

Now, after this unexpected invitation from Alik, we had a real dilemma facing us — should we go, or succumb to our cautious fear and not go? After all, the year was 1968, not 1958. We decided to go just out of curiosity, expecting to see a few Jews doing something Jewish.

As we were walking from the bus station toward the place called Synagogue, strange feelings started to emerge in my heart and head. My fear of being Jewish, my wish to always hide my Jewishness, my desire to blend into the crowd of Russians, and not to attract any attention to my identity as a Jew had become very natural to me until now. But at this moment, I was "coming out of the closet," so to speak, using the modern terminology. I am going where? Only Jews can walk in this direction and openly acknowledge their identity by walking with other Jews.

I was not at ease at all and was holding Sergei's hand very tight. We didn't know what to expect. *What if the KGB was waiting for all of us right there? We are volunteering to be arrested?* I looked around and to my absolute amazement I saw more and more people walking in the same direction. *They cannot all be Jews? No way... so many Jews?* I couldn't believe my eyes. This cannot be real! I had to pinch myself as we were getting closer and closer to the small yard surrounding the building called Synagogue.

It was packed with a young, vivacious crowd! Young men with guitars were playing some Jewish songs, and enthusiastic voices were joining them.

"We are Jews, Jews, and Jews, all around us only Jews."

It was an easy song to join and Sergei, my sister and I started singing loudly with all those people that we had never met before. We never imagined that there were so many of them, or rather of **us**. Our spirits were freed to participate in this new energy. It was contagious, accelerating. We tried to dance in circles some new kind of dance.

"It is Hora time," somebody screamed, and we got the bug right away. It felt so natural to hold hands and jump around in camaraderie, a closeness that I never felt before. I felt that I was among my own people for the first time in my life. I looked around — *Wow! They are all so young and beautiful, the men are so handsome, the girls are pretty. I don't belong to some ugly and subhuman group of people.* I felt some pride in my heritage for the first time in my life.

The small yard was becoming very overcrowded, as more and more people were coming in, that the celebration started to spill out into the streets. We were aware that the place was surrounded by police cars, but they were just watching us in amazement themselves. Never, ever had this been allowed in the U.S.S.R. before. The police did not expect the crowd to be so large, did not expect the crowd to be spilling onto the streets, and did not have instructions on how to deal with this new situation. They did not want for Russians to see any of this triumph of our Jewish spirit. The authorities themselves didn't know that it existed, but neither did we. I think that the police were just watching in hope for all this embarrassment to end as soon as possible and without some unexpected incident.

But Jews are not a violent crowd. No vodka was circulating around; we were just dancing and dancing, pretending that we were free to do it at least for this one time. I think that a few were arrested just to show that the police were still in power, but were let go fairly soon. As the night was winding down, the police were telling us that it was time to stop and go home. I wished they would just shut up and let us do it on our terms. Nobody wanted this event to end. We felt so happy, elated, in the clouds, and didn't have any desire to come back to reality.

It was hard to comprehend why, for all those years, the Soviet officials would make it a crime to live as Jews, to keep our traditions, to celebrate our holidays, to learn some history, to sing Jewish songs and dance together? But something was changing; a new energy was creeping in. The bug that we caught during this *Simchat-Torah* would not go away and would stay with us for years to come. It woke us up to a completely different reality and sparked our interest into the fascinating world of being a Jew and the far away land, called Israel.

We still had no idea that in just two years, we would hear for the first time from Sergei's friend Eizer that he and his family were planning to leave the Soviet Union and to go to Israel. In the meantime, during those two years our daughter Anechka was born, and our life was fully engaged around her. Nothing predicted to us the drastic and dramatic changes that Eizer's astonishing announcement would bring to our lives.

CHAPTER ELEVEN

We are back in our room in Haifa, after the signal of the siren ended. Danger was hopefully over, for now. Anechka is fast asleep. Sergei and I are mortified, looking at each other, lost in this strange place, not knowing what to think or what to do. We are completely confused, bewildered, wishing that somebody would take time to explain to us what this story is all about. We don't understand their language and can't understand the news. At home we never listened to the radio news, because it all was just lies, but here everybody is glued to the radio.

We cannot sleep. Sergei is very pale, trying to make some sense of the last events but I just feel awful, sick to my stomach, thinking, what a horrible situation we have gotten ourselves into and most of all wondering and worrying about my family at home. How is Mama after hearing the Russian news about this war in Israel? I wish we could call them, talk with them, let them know, that we are still alive and unharmed. I am scared; I know for sure that Mama, like all others of her generation, is in an absolute panic and maybe has even been hospitalized, considering all her heart problems.

We feel exhausted, lying in our bed, dressed, hugging each other, and waiting for the possible siren again. Maybe we'll get some information in the morning? It's just a couple more hours... I fall asleep at dawn, keeping myself as close to Sergei as possible — he is our protector, no matter what. The future is so bleak... Somebody wants to kill Jews, even in their own country? Is it out of the same *hate* again?? I thought that if Jews were living separately from all others, nobody would hate them anymore. Why? My head is spinning as I lose myself for a couple of hours in a heavy sleep.

I didn't want to wake up in the morning and face the reality of the new day. Sergei insisted on going down to the common area to talk with people, to figure out what was going on, to get some information. We met some people for the first time. Everyone looked extremely concerned, talking quietly with each other, asking questions with no answers. More people came. Some came from visiting their families in different parts of Israel. They had more information, as they spoke Yiddish to their relatives and got some ideas about what was going on. As they shared it with us, we gained a vague understanding.

Rumors started to circulate around us, one scarier than another. The situation is very dangerous. The war began as an absolute surprise attack by the Egyptian army. Israel is not prepared; they did not expect the attack. Syria is involved, too. Everything is getting out of hand. The Soviets are involved with supplying Egypt with weapons by air and sea. It can be a total defeat and the scariest of all the rumors —

"Did you hear that Israel has an atomic bomb??"

"Are they going to use it??"

What will happen to us? I thought. *Why are we even here? Nobody told us anything about any danger before. I don't want to be part of any war!! Why are they fighting? What is the reason?*

For one week I had felt like we had come to the Middle-Eastern heaven. I felt good about our decision to go through hell to get here, and the future was promising for the first time in our life. But what is happening now is a nightmare, a real catastrophe. Enemies, whoever they are, want to destroy and conquer Israel and to kill Jews? Again?

New names that we barely ever heard before, surfaced: Golda Meir, Moshe Dayan, Anwar Sadat, Saddam Hussein in Iraq (who apparently sent rockets to Haifa at night), Henry Kissinger and Richard Nixon. These were new players on the stage of our lives upon whom we were now depending. Our feelings were that Israel was incompetent and the government was weak and arrogant. *How could they be so negligent, not to be ready for war??*

Stalin did it in Russia, hiding the real situation from the Soviet people before World War II, but we understood why. There was no analogy that we could find, and no explanations fit this unraveling situation.

I listened attentively to the different ideas of various people. It was strange to find myself so unworldly, not prepared for the world beyond the

Kremlin wall. All our problems there were very simple for us to understand. We learned how to read between the lines, not to believe anything that anybody was saying or preaching, to see the division between the masses and ourselves, to see the goals of the Soviet government, the deceit, the disregard of the needs and desires of the people.

"One hand washes another," my father would say while explaining to me how the Communist Soviet government works. But here is a new world. *Who is washing the hands of whom? How does Israeli society work? Who dropped the ball? How could they be so ill prepared, when they were so great just a few years prior during the Six-Day War?* I thought that Israeli soldiers did a remarkable job in 1967. Russians were surprised and furious back then. What suddenly happened?

In the midst of all this chaos, I just wanted to find a way to get to the post office and to send a telegram home and let my family know that we were okay, that we were still alive. I was worried sick about both us and them. With the help of a nice girl who worked at the office of the *ulpan*, I was able to do this and relax a little bit afterward.

There were no more sirens going on and emotions started to calm down. We realized that fighting was going on at the defensible borders, not in proximity to Israel's heartland. That's a different kind of war so far, not like Russian wars.

After a couple of days, a few of our men decided that it was time to volunteer and to go to the army officials with a request to participate in the defense of Israel. They thought that the Israeli army needed help and more people to fight. The women agreed, thinking that it was a good idea. If we happened to be here in such a critical moment, our husbands should fight, too. A group of our men left after saying goodbye to us, and we were waiting for them to be accepted into the military. It is almost funny looking back and understanding that there was no way the Israeli army would accept those untrained and unprepared Russian civilians, who had never even held a weapon in their hands, into their elite forces. After a few hours, these men returned and told us that the army politely rejected their help at this moment. I was happy to see Sergei back with me, but we were all somewhat disappointed, feeling useless at this apocalyptic time.

A couple of weeks later, the Israeli army turned this fight into an overwhelming military victory. We heard the news from people around us that the Americans had helped. We heard that Golda Meir had convinced Nixon to deliver all the necessary weapons, and so it appears that there will be no nukes this time. I heard someone say,

"Thank God, it's over!"

I thought that Israel should probably thank America. After all, what has this victory to do with God?

It was a time for relief of unbearable tension not only for us, but for the whole country.

CHAPTER TWELVE

During the time of the Yom Kippur War, I barely slept. My mind was not able to relax, even for a moment, and the memories and images of my childhood and my parents' stories of the war that they went through circulated in my head and before my eyes.

I was a miracle child of the most horrendous war of all time. My parents were married on November 7, 1940. Ironically, that was also a day of a big celebration of the twenty-third anniversary of the October Revolution in the Soviet Union with all the pomp and circumstance for which the Russians were so famous.

On this day, year after year, there always was a huge military parade in Moscow's Red Square, presenting the glory and strength of the Soviet Army. In other cities there were huge demonstrations of "exultant citizens" showing their happy solidarity and support to the Communist Party and their leaders. Mostly, it was done to proclaim the love and adoration of the masses for their Dear Leader, Comrade Iosif Vissarionovich Stalin, who had only one competitor in the world arena for the better show — Adolf Hitler in Germany.

I think my parents chose this date for the holiday atmosphere and the bright energy. They also felt some reverence and appreciation for the opportunities given to them by the new regime. Most of all, it gave them an extra free day for their special occasion. The country, including my parents, certainly did not expect that they had only a little more than six months of happiness and peace before World War II would burst into their lives.

They were young and naïve, the first ones in their families to be allowed by the new Soviet regime to leave the *shtetls* (small Jewish villages) and to move to the big cities. They both grew up in Belorussia and after finishing high school, were ready to fly away from home to the wonderful city of

Leningrad to start an exciting journey on untouched ground — the equality of Jews in the new Soviet Union.

They were each accepted into different colleges. My father became a geologist, and my mother graduated as a financial economist. They met at a party given by my father's closest cousin Meyer and fell in love. Both were ready for a good, simple life. They acquired one of three neglected small horse stables on the back side of a big apartment complex from the local government, worked very hard to transform it into their somewhat livable nest, and expected to live happily ever after.

Both of my parents were apolitical. I think their energy went mostly to build their life in Leningrad and to adjust to the new environment, living among *goyim* (non-Jews) and trying to be like them. They changed their names to sound Russian. Pesia became Polina, and Isaac became Alexander or Sasha. They spoke only Russian now, not Yiddish, and tried to be and behave like the Russians around them. They had almost everything ready for a happy life, and a child — *Me* — was probably in their plans for the nearest future. Isn't that how life is supposed to go for most of us?

Their sweet and simple story just ended there. On June 22, 1941, the dream world of my parents came to an end and blended inexorably with the story of the entire world.

Of course they, like all other people of the huge Soviet Empire, were aware of the war that had started in 1939, had heard Hitler's name, and had some scarce information about Germany, Czechoslovakia, and Poland. But their "Father Stalin" told them to trust him. He would take care of everybody. Not to worry, he would prevent bad things from happening to them. He would protect Mother Russia. Everyone was supposed to go about their day-to-day life and work as hard as they could to build the best socialistic country in the world. And so, millions of people were just gullible believers.

The masses adored Comrade Iosif Vissarionovich Stalin for his leadership ability, strength and inspiring ideas. He projected full protection for his people under his safety net.   He could do no harm. He was their Teacher, their God, and their love toward him was unprecedented. It had no boundaries. They did not expect any drastic changes. Hitler and Stalin had negotiated the Nazi-Soviet Non-Aggression Pact, so in 1939 most of the people trusted those leaders and did not envision any problems for the next ten years.

Oh, the smooth and reassuring words of the communists that placate the souls of the masses while leading them carefully down to hell!

CHAPTER THIRTEEN

On June 22, 1941, suddenly the world that my parents lived in was turned upside down.

Germany declared war against Russia in the middle of a beautiful summer day. Unprepared, the naïve and politically uneducated masses had no idea about Hitler's plans to conquer the world, in which Russia played a vital role. Hitler hated Russians and considered them to be sub-humans. He hated Stalin and communism. He hated Jews the most, many of whom lived in Russia. Germans were intent on destroying the Soviet army and taking Moscow before the winter. Meanwhile, Stalin was trying desperately to rebuild his army following the 1930 putsches, when he had eliminated his senior officers through imprisonment or execution. This was described as "just a friendly cleansing of the staff." Heads rolled because of Stalin's personal paranoia, fear of competition as well as his hate toward anyone's tactical or political disagreements with the Leader.

There was not enough time to be ready for the most atrocious and evil war in the history of humanity. And so *Operation Barbarossa* was launched by Hitler against a desperately unprepared Red Army. But Hitler may have underestimated a basic and unique Russian character trait: their unprecedented deep patriotism, pride, and love for Mother Russia. The Russians united their forces in order to survive the Great Patriotic War, as they called it. The whole country rose up as one to defend their homeland. Nothing on earth could daunt Mother Russia.

My father and mother were among those who were shocked and unprepared. They were Jewish-Russian patriots at this point and they had no other homeland. Papa immediately decided to go and enlist in the Red Army as a volunteer, disregarding the fact that he was working at the railroad company as an engineer and thus could have been exempted from military service. He hugged and kissed his young wife goodbye and left her alone for the most trying experiences of her life. Immediately, my father was sent to defend his city of Leningrad, but the soldiers were ill-equipped, untrained, and despite their enthusiasm, hundreds were soon wounded or killed. My father was gravely wounded. A bullet pierced his throat, but not deeply enough to be fatal.

He was brought back to a hospital in Leningrad, and somehow my mother received word of his injury (I have no understanding how communications worked during the war without all our electronic devices). In any case, she walked many miles, since public transportation did not work, to see her wounded husband. She was astonished to see so many rows of men lying down on beds and on the floor, in the rooms, and mostly in the corridors. Although she searched desperately for him, she was unable to find her husband among the hundreds of men, many screaming from pain and begging for help.

She had actually walked past him a few times without recognizing him among the others. Finally, the nurse showed her a man with his head mostly covered with bandages. She believed that it was her husband, although she was stunned and could barely recognize him. Just one month of fighting in the war had completely changed his appearance. He had lost a lot of weight; food was scarce and severely limited. The color of his face was absolutely gray, and he was in a lot of pain, but his exhausted eyes looked at her with the same love and tenderness as before. Every evening after a day of work, she would walk many miles to the hospital to visit her husband and to attend to his recovery. My parents were so young at this time and so much in love, wishing that this nightmare somehow would disappear and the world would leave them alone to continue to live their happy lives.

Though they may have believed that this moment was the worst of their problems, they would soon find out that this was just the beginning.

The minute Papa felt better, he was ordered back to the fields of war, leaving Mama alone for the second time in just a few months. I can only imagine this scene, full of tragic sadness, tears of real despair, hugging each other possibly for the last time. They had lost their innocence. Now it was not about patriotism; it was about life and death.

It was excruciatingly difficult for them to separate, to stop hugging, kissing and saying goodbye. They both realized that there was a very high probability that he was going to die. Papa was also very concerned that he was not leaving even a child, maybe a son who would carry on his name. He could just disappear without a trace. His young life could be over in this horrible war, and for what? His Polina had to be left behind without any protection in the city, without support of the family, with only a couple of friends, mostly just co-workers. He promised her that he would overcome all the adversities he would face, he would be strong, and he would come back home alive. "I am not going to die. I promise, I'll be back." These were his last words to his young wife as they parted, with tears in their eyes and love for each other in their hearts. Neither of them knew that *her* chances of dying would soon become much greater than even *his*.

My mother learned later that when my father returned to the army, he, being a geologist, was sent to the most dangerous artillery division to become a mine officer.

"Do you know what this means?" he would ask me many years later in one of our very rare conversations about the war.

"Ten soldiers would go to check the mine fields and maybe one would come back alive."

"So this one always would be you, Papa?" I asked.

He smiled at me with his mysterious and intriguing smile.

"Remember, Ellochka, I was seriously wounded twice. But I survived."

I had the strangest feeling throughout my life that I kept as my secret from everybody. I deeply believed that before I was born, my sister and I were our parents' guardian angels. We chose them to be our parents and we were helping to keep them alive against all odds. Otherwise, they would have had absolutely zero chance to survive...

CHAPTER FOURTEEN

The siege of Leningrad began on September 8, 1941. Until then, Mama had been living alone in her apartment and working as an economist for the local government. This day changed her life and the lives of the people of the city for the next nine hundred days. Hitler's goal was to wipe Leningrad from the face of the earth. Their main weapon against the citizens was complete starvation. German and Finnish forces from the North surrounded the city, cutting off all supply routes to the city of Leningrad, which was absolutely not prepared for the war. Food storage warehouses were lacking provisions, but the communist party chief lied to Stalin, telling him that the warehouses were full, so several relief food trains were diverted elsewhere. In addition, every evening, precisely at the same time, German airplanes were bombarding and destroying the most vital locations in the city from the air. They destroyed the warehouses containing food first, leaving no provisions at all. Sirens would go off all through the city, and people would run to the shelters.

Mama told me later that at first, she ran with everybody as fast as she could, but as time went on and she became tired, cold, depressed, weak, and mostly hungry, she stopped paying attention and ignored the sirens altogether. Every morning she would force herself to go to work — that was a requirement for everyone who was still alive. Many times co-workers would stay on top of the roof of their work buildings after the air bombardment, to defuse bombs that did not explode and bring them down into sand boxes to prevent fires, a dangerous job by all means. She also was mobilized with everyone else, who was still standing, to construct fortifications around the city. After work hours she would stay in bed in the darkness, shivering, her teeth rattling, covering herself with as many blankets as she could find, but still shivering. The walls of the apartment were covered with a thick layer of frost. She had no energy left, no desire to move and later, even no fear.

The winter of 1941-42 was one of the coldest in the recorded history of Leningrad. In the midst of these extreme temperatures, the basic municipal services did not work. There was no electricity or heating, and neither the water supply nor public transportation worked. No food was available, except for a daily ration of 125-200 grams of bread made mostly out of sawdust and other inedible ingredients, which was distributed to those with ration cards at workplaces. At first, Mama, among others, would walk to the shore of the Neva River with buckets to get some drinking water through the holes that had been cut in the ice. But with the passage of time, nobody had any energy left for those far away, icy trips. It was mostly the elderly, women, and children who lived in the city; all the younger men had gone to war. Mothers would give their bread to their children and the mothers would die first, followed soon after by their children.

"I, at least, didn't have children to suffer with me and had a little piece of this surrogate bread to myself. You know, Ellochka, in the beginning of the blockade, when we saw people dying on the streets, we would run to help, trying to hold them, to help them to get up. We would put corpses on the sleds and bring them to burial areas. But with time, we got used to this picture, and did not have any strength or even a desire to help. Apathy kicked in, inertia, depression, and indifference. Corpses would just pile up and accumulate on the streets. The time comes, as you stop caring, feeling or thinking, that you start losing your humanity. Hunger is your worst enemy. Nothing can be compared to starvation, not even fear. I lost most of my weight and was just 'skin and bones,'" Mama would tell me, preventing me and my sister from ever leaving anything on our plates or God forbid, to throw pieces of old bread into the garbage. Food, and especially bread, was always treated by my mother as a real treasure all through the remaining days of her life.

"Rumors of cannibalism were circulating around, and they were true," my mother told me once, when I got older and pressured her to tell me the truth.

"People ate unimaginable things: birds, rats, and pets. I did not, just because I was extremely squeamish and fastidious all my life. I never ate a lot anyway and I was young. I just suffered quietly. But I would take pieces of the wallpaper with paste or glue on it to the workplace, where electricity was working, and we could boil some water. We would cook soup made from the wallpaper paste and would be bewildered, and wonder why we did not eat such a delicious soup before the war!"

There was a wave of thievery of food and ration cards. A few times the piece of bread would be stolen from Mama, and that would bring her to tears and despair. Thank God she never lost her ration card, since that would be a death sentence. Ration cards were irreplaceable.

People did not wash for months, since, obviously, the bath-houses did not work. They could not wash their clothes.

"Nobody ever smiled," Mama said.

In addition to all the other disasters, my Mama, like some other Jews, had a capsule of poison in her possession, given to her by the government official at her work. She was told to use it immediately in case the Germans entered the city. I guess Stalin didn't want to complicate Hitler's life by transferring those Russian Jews to the camps. It would be easier to finish them off right away; but this is just my conclusion.

I think my Mama never lost her heart and soul in the midst of this sadistic atmosphere. She could have given up and just died, but like many survivors in the concentration camps, her soul wanted to survive, no matter what.

CHAPTER FIFTEEN

There were no evacuation plans available in the chaos of the first year of the war. The city was in absolute isolation until the following winter of 1942.

The ice road over Lake Ladoga, sometimes called the Road of Life, became available to bring some food in and take some people out. Leaving Leningrad was a very dangerous proposition. Some people walked, others used old decrepit vehicles that moved slowly along the ice road one after another, and sometimes got stuck in the snow or sank through the broken ice. The Germans were precisely and constantly bombarding the road. Just a lucky few survived to reach the other side. Consequently, people also called it the Road of Death.

I think the time had come for my sister and me to save our parents, although we were still waiting to be born.

As Mama was contemplating a plan to escape with some help from her devoted friends, Papa was seriously wounded a second time. A bullet or bomb part hit his back, only a couple of centimeters from his spinal cord. As he was lying in the hospital with minimal chance of survival, somewhere in the heart of Russia, my Mama found a way to escape from the hell that she had lived in for so long. This is where their story becomes extremely surreal and almost incomprehensible by our earthly measures.

I have so many questions about this short period of their life with no answers, only my imagination. What was wrong with me? Why did I never ask them the important details of their story to help me understand the situation? I guess our own lives take precedence over our family's history, and through our youth, the curiosity about our parents' lives is not very prevalent. Until one day, our parents are gone, and so many fascinating stories are gone with them...

I only know a few facts about this period of my parents' lives. They met somewhere on the crossroads of this most lethal war in history. Mama was just out of the horror of starvation and had somehow passed across the Road of Death, where there was almost no chance of survival. Papa was barely out of the hospital after his horror of serving as a lieutenant in the most dangerous division of the Red Army, where he had received many medals for his bravery and great service to his country.

They had not seen each other for a couple of years, and hardly could recognize each other. She was suffering from starvation, looked like a skeleton and had just started slowly to eat some long-forgotten food. He was barely moving after having been severely wounded a second time. They spent a little time together in the middle of nowhere… It is a great story for a sentimental movie, but in real life? It is hard to believe, but the truth is, she was pregnant with *ME* before he was sent back to the front. She didn't know it yet when they were saying goodbye to each other.

It breaks my heart to envision them embracing each other in tears for the last time, whispering words of true love, devotion and hope. I can see them glued together in the deepest sorrow, afraid to move, to separate, to break this moment. I wanted to scream to them from the future,

"It will be all right after all. You will survive, my dear parents, because I will be looking after you."

I only know that in real life, we cannot imagine that things would happen in this way. My mother and father had beaten all odds to still be alive, when they had a near zero chance to remain alive. The odds against me being conceived at this time were astronomical. Women stopped menstruating during the siege of the city for lack of body fat, basic nutrition and hygiene.

This was a miraculous conception by any measure.

CHAPTER SIXTEEN

After my father's departure for the front, somehow my mother traveled through Russia to get to the Ural Mountains that divide the European and Asian parts of Russia. My Babushka Meita, Dedushka (grandpa) Benzion, Mama's younger sister Ida and her older sister Fania, with two young children, had been living there since the beginning of the war.

I was always amazed by my grandpa Benzion's decision to literally run away from the Germans. He was a soldier during World War I and was taken prisoner. He came back home distrusting everybody, especially Germans. When the new war broke out, he told my babushka to start packing a few necessities.

"We are leaving Rogachev right away," he insisted. She didn't want to go.

"Why, Benzion, should we run away? Nobody else is running. All my family is staying, no one in the whole Jewish community is even thinking about it, and the rabbis are not telling us to run!"

"I am sorry, Meita, but I cannot put my head on their shoulders. I understand what is coming and nobody wants to listen. They just want to put their heads into the sand and continue praying. Well, you will see, it won't help them. You'll see, terrible things will start happening here very soon, and then they will remember me and the warnings I gave them, but it will be too late. Just trust me, Meita, say goodbye to your family and wish them well. We must leave right away!"

Babushka didn't know what to believe. Her immediate family was not willing to move. Her dear sister Havah thought that Benzion was just panicking for no reason, as usual, and that Meita should finally put her foot down.

"He hasn't been a good provider for you and the family. I do not think you should follow him. Look, so many people believe that we'll be safe here and we'll survive just fine, being together here in our *shtetl*. Where does he want us to go? This is our home, our life. What is the worst that could happen to us? So the Germans would come and we'll live under the Germans. What is the difference for us? They don't want to harm civilians like us. We are just little people going about our lives, and we'll pray to God for help, if we would ever need it."

Sometimes, I wish I had been there by my Dedushka Benzion's side, screaming at those Jews:

"How could you be so short-sighted, stubborn, stiff-necked and not even try to fathom the prophecy of my grandpa?"

They all paid an unbelievably heavy price: torture and horrific death. Their *shtetl* of Rogachev was occupied at the beginning of July 1941. The Nazis did not hide their intention, which was the massacre of all the Jews. The Ghettos were opened in Belorussia, the Jews were required to wear yellow stars, and the killings started right away, first in smaller groups and later with mass murders. By March 1942, 3,500 Jews had been killed and buried in mass graves in Rogachev alone. And all of our extended family perished. All together, 90 percent of the Jews in Belorussia had been murdered, more than three million people. Only a few survived by joining the Russian resistance underground groups. They were called Partisans.

But my grandpa understood the situation and insisted on leaving their home before the tragedy unfolded. It was not an easy journey, walking many kilometers in the hot weather, and then sailing on an open barge to Dnepropetrovsk, jumping into a railroad cement car, then walking again. There were three of them; Grandpa, Babushka and their younger daughter Ida, who was 13 years old. They finally reached their destination of the Ural Mountains after many arduous months of traveling. There they were reunited with their older daughter Fania and her two children, who lived there after having been evacuated from Leningrad.

The family had little information about Pesia, my Mama. They often thought that she was dead, since there was almost no communication. But to my absolute amazement the postal offices worked during the war, and somehow, my family members were connecting the dots.

∞

I love the next part of the story.

My Mama made it through the Road of Death and somehow made her way to the Ural Mountains. She finally appeared before her family in the middle of summer, being four months pregnant with ME. They hugged and kissed, cried and screamed, jumped and danced around from the happiness of being together again.

I can see those pictures clearly. The next scene is when they realized my mother's peculiar condition. Everyone is shocked; they cannot believe their eyes. Ida is curious, Fania is bewildered, and my babushka is the only one that looks excited and even happy. But my grandpa is furious.

"What is wrong with you, Pesia? In the middle of the war, after nearly starving to death? With a husband who could be killed any day? What were you both thinking? How can you bring a child into this hateful, *mishugene* (crazy) world? How can this child be born normal and not be an invalid? There's no nutrition, no food, no doctors. We are living in somebody else's house, out of their kindness, sleeping on the floor, and the war can go on for many more months! The only food here is half-rotten potatoes, and during the winter, it will be even worse!"

My poor Grandpa Benzion! I really can understand his anguish, despair and worries and I actually absolutely agree with him. But I hear Babushka trying to calm him down:

"Every child comes to this world bringing his own happiness." I love the wisdom of my babushka.

Listening to them from the other side, so to speak, I wanted to give them big hugs and assure them that by the end of the day everything will be all right, and it all will be worth it because it's ME, and I really want to be born, no matter what.

∞

By December 1943, Mama became big despite malnutrition and all her other poor conditions. She had to make some preparations. No babies had been born around there for almost three years. Grandpa Benzion was right about a lot of things in life! She finally found a small hospital many kilometers away. It was mostly closed, but the nurse, who lived not far away, would open the clinic in cases of emergency.

The winter weather was miserable, stormy, windy, and excruciatingly cold. The only way to get to the hospital was by using a horse with a sled. They borrowed a horse, but nobody knew anything about horses, especially how to coax one to pull a sled. When the big day came and I was preparing to enter the world, my Mama's sisters helped her into the sled, and then they climbed in and pulled on the reins. After a while, it got to be really hard. There was an enormous amount of snow, and wolves were howling all around. What an awfully scary journey for everyone, including me, but mostly for my Mama. A couple of times, they overturned the sled and found themselves, including my poor laboring Mama, in the ditches. Thinking about it now, it is kind of funny, but I am sure it was not at all funny at the time.

It took them a long time to finally get to the hospital, which was closed. It was late and dark, and my mom was in a lot of pain, barely keeping herself from crying. The nurse finally came and opened the door. The room was cold, the same temperature as outside, and there was neither electricity nor hot water. I did not care much, but Mama was suffering, as her contractions were getting stronger and stronger. The nurse lit some candles and they all put their coats on top of my Mama so that she would stop shivering. She was crying, pushing, and screaming,

"It is so hard to give birth to one child, and Hitler is killing millions!"

I did not hear it or did not understand, but I do remember her telling this to me, when I got older.

I also remember that when I was in labor myself with Anechka. I thought, *What was my Mama screaming, when she was giving birth to me?* It seemed so strange to me, but not to my mother. She had such an unreal path, such an unbelievably difficult time to come to this point and to give birth to a new life. In any case I wanted to help her as much as I could all through labor, and it didn't take too long for my Mama and my aunts to hear my strong scream, announcing to the world my miraculous birth. I think I remember that it looked beautiful with all those candles around me, just very, very cold.

Mama, my dear Mama, I am forever grateful to you for giving me life and bringing me to this world in these inhumane conditions in that inhumane time. You are my hero and I will love you forever...

After a while a telegram came from my Papa:

"Congratulations with our Son. Love. Sasha."

He wanted to have a son to continue his name in case he would be killed. Papa just did not know that I had the power to save his life, even after I was born.

I was waiting to meet him for the next two years, before he finally came home from Germany, where he finished his service in this long, long war. Close to the end of the war, it was the first time he was allowed to cross the Soviet borders as an officer of the Red Army. He mentioned to me briefly, many years later, that entering Dresden in 1945 after the spring Allied bombings of the city was a heavy experience for him. Dresden was badly damaged, basically leveled and destroyed. This created conflicting feelings of justifiable revenge, but also the empty feelings of the horrific war violence and crimes. Russian soldiers did not hold back their anger and hate for Germans and expressed it in atrocities toward the women of Dresden. My father said to me once that it was sickening for him to watch the display of the power of men in this terrible way. My father was a gentle man and tried to not dwell on those horrible years of the war. What was the end game for normal people? Papa did not see any gain in countries fighting with each other for political reasons. But he was proud of being part of defending his country and being honored with many medals for bravery and outstanding service. His most important objective was to survive, and he did.

My grandpa was not so lucky. He passed away from malnutrition six months after I was born. I didn't have the opportunity to get to know him, but I think about him often, with reverence. He would give my mother extra food from his portion of potatoes and bread, knowing that she was nursing me. Many years of suffering and wars had weakened his body. He was only 65 years old. I think he loved having me around. I brought life to their miserable existence, hope for a better future, and hope that maybe, just maybe their lives were not lived in vain. I would like to think that I received some of his spark to understand this world and to make my decisions in life according to the ideals of my dear grandpa Benzion Farberov. My hope is that during my life, some of my decisions and actions would make him proud of *Me*, his war-baby granddaughter.

CHAPTER SEVENTEEN

Right after her father's death, Mama decided to head back home to Leningrad. She had to go back to work to be able to feed me, and care for her other family members. She was afraid that somebody would move into her apartment, and she would have no place to reside. The state required certain documents and permission to enter the city of Leningrad, which was closed for non-residents. Babushka did not have papers to enter the city. Nevertheless, Mama decided to take a risk. On the overcrowded train she made Babushka lie down underneath some covers and blankets and put me on the top. I helped my Babushka to get through the checkpoint. Since everybody was enchanted and amused, seeing a beautiful baby, such a rarity in wartime, the overtired controllers forgot their duties and did not act suspiciously. It was a great break for all of us and I felt important for the first time in my life.

The Siege of Leningrad ended on January 27, 1944. One third of the population, or about one million people, had died from starvation, exposure, and artillery shelling from German positions outside of the city, fires, air bombs or diseases. Only 700 children were born in 1943 (and most of them died anyway), compared to over 175,000 born in 1939. Later, in school, we always had the lowest number of students in our classes. We were a rare group of people — children of wartime.

Much of the infrastructure had been destroyed by air raids and artillery. By the end of the Siege, it was a ghost city. Survivors started to come back in February, 1944. They immediately began rebuilding and repairing the ruined industries, schools, and hospitals. We came back in June, 1944, straight to our miserable apartment, the one in which Mama had lived through the horror of war. I brought life and energy back to this place, but it was certainly not an appropriate place for raising a child. Fortunately, I don't have memories of this time. It would be too depressing.

As I mentioned before, my father finally returned home in 1946, and my parents did not waste their time. My sister Larisa was born nine months later. What a great tribute to their strength, power and desire to be alive and to start their life again with a great spirit!

The first memory of my life (I was two years and ten months old) is when Papa and I went to bring my Mama and my little sister Larisa home from the hospital. I was in heaven, and I adored her right away. I called her Lala, which was easier for me to pronounce than Larisa, and her new name stuck for life. Having a younger sister was a gift from heaven. If not for Lala, I probably would have had a miserable childhood. We have been close friends throughout our lives and we have endured many challenges together.

When I grew up and heard some of my mother's rare and incredible stories of survival, many things did not make sense to me. All through my childhood, I had heard endless stories of heroism and patriotism of Leningrad, the Hero City that withstood Hitler's fights and yet did not fall. Such a glorified myth was hard for me to accept. I absolutely acknowledge, that all of the Leningraders, including my mother, were Heroes, trying to withstand all the atrocities of the inhumane situation that they found themselves in. But mostly, they were victims of the unprecedented barbarism and savagism of one of the most so-called cultured people on earth at that time.

Looking back from the 21st century, I only can break my head trying to understand how these atrocities were ever possible among humans. We cannot just blame everything on Adolf Hitler, but also on so many aspiring "little Hitlers" in so many countries. Apparently, cruelty is in our blood, in our human DNA. It is just covered up until somebody's match is lit to start the fire.

I always felt that if Hitler had decided to enter the city and conquer it, nothing would have stopped him at that time in 1941. I thought Hitler's decision was to not spend much energy on Leningrad so that all the people would just starve to death. It was a cruel genocide of the masses. I realized the truth only after moving to the West. I read somewhere those words:

"The Fuhrer has decided to have Leningrad wiped off the face of the earth," according to his generals. I was right to never trust Soviet versions of history and propaganda. Ever...

Stalin's version was different. He saw himself as a Hero and a brilliant general who saved Leningrad and the entire U.S.S.R. from the disasters of the war. According to my father and other soldiers, war books and some Soviet propaganda movies, all the soldiers were always screaming at the top of their lungs "For our Stalin, for our homeland!!" as they were running to attack their enemies during battles. They were ready to die for *him?*

For years afterward, Stalin kept the real story of the Siege in darkness. The death toll was underestimated. His version was that the citizens sacrificed their lives to defend the cradle of the revolution (that's how propaganda works). In reality, Stalin never liked or trusted Leningrad — it had too much culture, too many intellectuals who deserved to be killed, and perhaps some undetected opposition. He had contempt toward the leaders of the city, because they were becoming too popular among the people. He never wanted to share his glory with anyone else. So in 1950, he falsely accused Leningrad's party leaders of some kind of treason. Many were eliminated and others were imprisoned. Papa was always saying,

"It's just a fight for power. The strong ones will finish the weak."

Stalin was not eager to help to rebuild Leningrad. He gave the money to other cities, such as Stalingrad, and directed more wealth toward Moscow and away from Leningrad. The redistribution of wealth and elimination of so-called enemies was a strategy of Generalissimo Comrade Stalin based on the principles of his teachers Karl Marx and Vladimir Lenin. He was in power to make all the decisions for the stupid people, so that the younger generation, that I was part of, would be raised to become "animals in the zoo." Nevertheless, we loved growing up in the cultural center of the U.S.S.R., and always felt privileged to live there, compared to any other place, for the very reasons that Stalin hated our city.

The war was finally over on May 9, 1945, with millions and millions of people dead all over the world. What was accomplished, which goals were reached, how many lives and countries were destroyed? Who benefited and for what? None of this ever made sense to me.

The Russians' losses were staggering, but they strongly believed that they had not only won the war and saved Mother Russia, but had also saved the entire world. We barely heard in our schools about the help of the Second Front and the Americans' participation in the war, except that Mama would tell me that the canned food donated by the Americans was very helpful and tasty. For a short time, there was a big celebration with fireworks, music and hugs between strangers on the streets of Leningrad. And soon after this celebration, Stalin resumed his own war and purges on his own enemies, continuously destroying and ruining the lives of innocent people in the U.S.S.R.

Unfortunately, my sister and I, together with many other children, were born in an unhappy, evil country, where hate prevailed. The greatest lie of the communist propaganda was that the U.S.S.R. was built on love and friendship of all the collective republics. In reality, they all hated each other. All I knew was that the Polish hated the Russians and Ukrainians, the Ukrainians hated the Russians, and all the other republics of the U.S.S.R. hated each other. Later, I realized that the European countries also despised each other, although maybe not with the same intense viciousness that the Germans had. The only common denominator among all of them is that collectively, they all hated Jews all the time.

Chapter Eighteen

O h, Israel, my love and my pain, my amazement and my concern. Israel, the place where I felt at home for the first time in my life, but as things eventually turned out, I could not stay there and had to leave. Israel, the sacred place where my soul belongs, but not during this lifetime...

The Yom Kippur war was over, and our normal life of the *olim hadashim* (new emigrants) began. Anechka (whose name had been changed to the Jewish version, Hanna or Hanele) and a few other children her age from our *ulpan* were placed into a local preschool, where everybody spoke only Hebrew. She loved it there, and in a couple of months she was fluent in children's Hebrew. We adults were not as lucky. Learning a new language was hard at first, and we were worried about our future. How in the world would we be able to go to work in only four months?

We went to our classes every day and studied very seriously. Our teacher was the best we could have possibly had. The whole group loved her very much, and she became our connection and introducer to this new world called Israel. She worked with a great new system of teaching Hebrew and was very encouraging to us all. Strangely to us, her name was Sarah. In the U.S.S.R this name was symbolic of anti-Semitism toward women. The name Sarah was ridiculed and considered racist. No parents would ever give this name to a daughter. It was new for us to start getting accustomed to a different perspective on things. We made a few very good friends right away, and tried to open ourselves to a more positive outlook for our future. We were sheltered from the world outside of the *ulpan*, and still understood very little about our new homeland.

After the shock of the war, we could not stop thinking that this land was very problematic. We heard rumors that the Arabs, who apparently were our neighbors on all sides, wanted to throw Jews into the sea. I was sure that it was an exaggeration, but I could not understand what the dispute was all about. It was not comforting and we thought that another war could start at any time.

Sergei was very uncertain about our promise to my family to send them emigration documents right away. We did not know about the military situation in Israel before we left Russia, but now with this new knowledge and firsthand information, we had to make a decision for the rest of the family. Our friends informed us of a simple solution. Refugees from the U.S.S.R. could go straight to America from Vienna and would be welcomed there with pomp and circumstance. I did not know what to do; either solution seemed unacceptable. I would prefer for them to emigrate to America. Maybe it would be a better place, or at least more peaceful, but we really did not know anybody there and had no information on or connections to the United States, the most intriguing country in the world. Mostly, I didn't want to scare my mother with a new proposal that would split our families into two different countries.

Throughout my life I was worried about my mother's health and her ability to deal with more stress than she already had. With heavy hearts and a lot of soul searching and debates we sent them all necessary documents to come to Israel; at least our family would be together. At this time we could write letters to each other, but only with a lot of coded information. They learned how to read between the lines, so to speak. We braced ourselves for a waiting period, in hopes that the government would let them go. I had many doubts about our future, but couldn't wait for my family to get out of Russia.

Meanwhile, we started to wake up from our deep misconceptions and began figuring out a lot of new information. We were like sponges, like children discovering their new surroundings. Sergei was the best student in our Hebrew classes and started to question Sarah about life in Israel.

"Who is paying for our *ulpan*?"

"The American Jewish organizations," answered Sarah.

"Who is paying for our children's preschool?"

"American Jews."

We were interested to learn that Americans helped Russia to win World War II. I do not remember learning much about this in our history lessons. "They give us a lot of support and money. There are a lot of very wealthy American Jews who love Israel and are ready to help," Sarah would explain in simple Hebrew. We were so proud to be able to understand her answers. It also made us realize how poor and dependent the new country of Israel was on America at this time. It was very disconcerting, to say the least, since we had come from a country that proclaimed to be the strongest in the world.

A few things were very strange to us. We didn't feel any enthusiasm from the Israeli authorities toward the new emigrants. It seemed that they especially did not feel enthusiasm about *Russim* the way our friends told us the Americans felt. The director of our *ulpan* was a middle-aged woman from Romania and half of the emigrants were from Romania. Well, apparently Romanian Jews did not like Russian Jews. They looked down on us. The director placed the Romanians into the main building of the *ulpan* with much better accommodations and other privileges. Many Russians were upset. Sergei and I did not really care, but I did not expect to encounter any hard feelings among Jews! This feeling of being disliked as Russians was extremely hurtful. The last thing I wanted to experience was to be the wrong ethnicity again!

Later, when the time came for Sergei to start looking for a job, the negative sense of being *ole hadash mi Russia*, or a new emigrant from Russia, became even stronger. There was much tension between Jewish groups from different countries, who disliked each other for no apparent reason. It was our painful realization that there was animosity between Sephardic Jews (ethnic groups originating in Spain and Portugal) and Ashkenazim (from Central and Eastern Europe). Some *schwarze* (black) Jews from Arab countries, Africa, and some other places were supposedly not as superior as white Jews from Europe. We could not believe that this was happening in our new young country. Israel was only twenty-five years old and it would take many years until all Jews would become equal and blend together as one nation. I doubted that it would happen soon, and this was extremely upsetting and painful for Sergei and me. I think all of us want to live in a country where there is no animosity between people based on nationality or ethnicity. We had plenty of it in the U.S.S.R, but in Israel?

∞

While we were in the *ulpan*, we received an invitation for dinner from Ada and Shmerl. What a great treat it was for us to walk twenty minutes to their apartment and be greeted by the kindest old couple in the world. It was the first time since Uncle Yanek and Aunt Simone had flown back to Paris that we had left our *ulpan* and ventured out to visit real Israeli people.

They lived in a small but very charming place, and I loved it right away. The food they served us was very tasty, containing many unfamiliar spices, not our usual plain Russian cuisine that we were accustomed to. Ada was a great cook and a very warm hostess. Her style of preparing and serving food was so different from most Russians, including my mother, who never had time for culinary adventures with new recipes. Our food at home in Russia was mostly monotonous and repetitious. Lack of fresh vegetables, poor quality of produce, limited assortment, and absence of spices and influences of other world cuisines did not help to create a memorable dining experience for me. I, like many others Russians, certainly could not consider myself a connoisseur of delicious foods or wine. So Ada's dinner was my first discovery on the road to different cuisines of the world. I loved and appreciated it immediately.

Mostly, I was fascinated by their brief story of survival throughout the Holocaust. Like my parents, this stoic generation was reluctant to speak about their war experiences and tried not to dwell on the horrors of the past. Coming from Russia, we knew almost nothing about the Holocaust. The war stories that we heard were always about Russian suffering and sacrifice, Russian heroism and bravery, Russian victories. All other nation-alities were mentioned only briefly, and Hitler's concentration camps were described as international — for all the nations, including some Jews and Gypsies. As I was growing up, I did not hear or read about the six million Jews who perished according to Hitler's plan to eliminate this one group of people from the face of the earth. It was an official silence, a topic that was purposely untouched by comrade Stalin and the State. Also, there were no disclosures about the tremendous support from the Ukrainians and Polish police, who assisted the German army in the process of extermination of the entire population of Jews in the territories of Ukraine and Poland. This information was carefully and fearfully whispered from person to person. Our parents obviously knew much more on this subject than their children, including the horrific massacre of entire families of our relatives in Belorussia. But they could not bear to ever discuss it with us.

It was twenty years later when we finally learned of the horrors that our brothers and sisters had endured. Ada and Shmerl, our new family in Haifa, came out of the ashes of Auschwitz, having lost all their relatives, parents, spouses, and children. Somehow, they miraculously survived. They met right after the war in the temporary transit camp, got married and never separated from each other. Israel became their home in 1949, one year after the establishment of Israeli Independence. They belonged to a very special group called *vaticim*, or old inhabitants.

As time passed by and our Hebrew improved, we began to understand and imagine much better what those wonderful people went through. And every time I heard their stories, my heart would almost stop beating from the unimaginable horrors dear Ada and Shmerl had endured in their lives. All other problems and obstacles in our life suddenly became much smaller and less significant. I had a strong desire to do something very special for this sweet couple, to bring some joy to them, to find some special words of comfort. In my own way, I honored them by asking Shmerl to become a *sandek*, a special person who holds the baby on his knees, during my son Jacob's *Bris* ceremony in 1975.

Our time in the *ulpan* was coming to an end. Our Hebrew was good enough to have a simple conversation, and supposedly, we were ready to start life on our own. By now, Anechka spoke Hebrew to us, liked her preschool, and knew a lot of songs. She seemed to be a very happy child and had quickly forgotten any episodes of the past.

One of the things that most impressed Sergei and I was to see Israeli couples our age in the parks or on the streets with three or four children, with the next one on the way. It was a revolutionary idea for me. *So many children? In one family? How is it possible? How can they afford it? Where do they all sleep? Who is taking care of them?*

In Russia, most of the couples would have only one child, and would almost never risk having another one. The living conditions were so difficult, the financial situation so bad, and raising even one child was so challenging. No diapers, no baby food, no breast pumps, no separate bedroom for the child. We had to walk a very long distance in any weather, snow or rain, to the baby's center for yogurt, which was the only food allowed by doctors to give to the babies. It took so much effort to raise even one child.

But here in Israel, young mothers looked content, happy, and beautiful in their bright, colorful special outfits. I admired the possibilities, but needed a little more time to adjust to these new ideas.

CHAPTER NINETEEN

Suddenly, the greatest news came from my family. They had received permission to leave the U.S.S.R., and were given only couple of weeks to get out! We never expected such a fast decision on the government's part, but it was the beginning of a new year, 1974, and they needed large numbers of Jews to leave Russia to get their needed grain for the starving Communists. *Wow!!*

This was one of the happiest days of my life. Who would have believed that I would see my parents, my sister and Mark, and little Mishenka only six months after we had parted? Unbelievable, a miracle, only possible in the scripted movies! This wonderful news lifted my spirits to the highest level. I couldn't stop smiling, jumping around and dancing with Anechka, telling her that her Babushka and Dedushka would come to be with her very soon and we would never separate again, ever.

On the second day of February we were all hugging each other in the Israeli International airport at Lod. Our emotions were at the highest level of incredulity, joy, happiness and pure euphoria. It was a warm day, but they all were dressed in wintery Russian coats and boots. They left a cold, cold Russia to never look back or feel nostalgia about this God-forsaken place that had created such a devastating life for all of us. My Mama and Papa finally were close to me; I could touch them, talk with them, cry, and laugh with them. We all were out of the danger zone, and we were ready for the next chapter of our life.

Sochnut, the Jewish Immigration agency, wanted to send them to Beer-Sheva, but we had taught our family through our letters to demand placement closer to Haifa. We already knew that the Jews in power in Israel were not always using their power sensibly, to say it mildly, but in fact quite the opposite. Those in power were very arrogant, insensitive, and inconsiderate — surprise, surprise! But Mark withstood their pressure and, after long negotiations finally got permission to go to beautiful Tivon, thirty minutes away from Haifa. On this very high note our life began anew as a complete family again.

We immersed ourselves in the waters of day-to-day life, trying to swim with all our power, to find our way and to understand the Israeli society and the rules of engagement, so to speak. Sergei was intensely but unsuccessfully looking for a job. He was an electrical engineer, but the economy was down and jobs were scarce. He didn't like the situation and was getting impatient to get out of the *ulpan*. Finally he got a break and found a very good job at Taasiat-Zvait, a government-run military company. Soon after he began his new career, we started to wait for our *Dira-Zmanit*, a temporary apartment that *Sochnut* was providing all the emigrants after completing their training at the *ulpan*.

Somehow, we got the most beautiful, newly built temporary apartment, the best in the whole city of Haifa in the prestigious area of Romema Yeshanah. The apartment had three bedrooms with all the luxuries that we had never experienced before, with a breathtaking view from the hills of Carmel to a winding road downhill, surrounded by tall trees on both sides of the road. It was at this moment that Sergei and I decided to add another child to our family. What a great decision it was! I felt like I was in a foreign movie again, experiencing the happiest days of my entire life. I was pregnant with my second child, with my son Jacob. I knew that I would have a son right away, because it was a completely different pregnancy from the start.

There are a few moments in everyone's life, when we feel blessed beyond all our dreams and expectations, beyond our understanding and intuition, the feeling of being in Seventh Heaven, in Nirvana, in the Garden of Eden, in Wonderland. It seemed like heaven suddenly opened up and showered us with blessings. It was the highest point of my entire life and I just wish I would have known to thank God for those blessings, to praise God for giving me this divine break and divine providence. I still had no awareness about God, but subconsciously, I had the feeling of some divine intervention and the divine presence that helped me once and again to reach for the stars in my personal journey. Sergei felt the same way and we both were drinking from the well of absolute bliss for a while. My entire family experienced these feelings; we all felt this way. I remember telling my Mama about my pregnancy for the first time, and her face lit up with pure happiness and joy.

Wow, we had come such a long way out of darkness and were anticipating years of light ahead of us.

CHAPTER TWENTY

I didn't have a choice for my future son's name.

"According to Jewish tradition, he will be named Yakov Okun, like my father," Sergei explained. I never met my father-in-law; he died a long time before we were married. But Sergei's mother Tosca was a part of our life and actually we were waiting for her and Serge's brother Victor to arrive in Israel within the next few months.

I did not have an easy time communicating with my mother-in-law, but I had tremendous respect for her, especially knowing her life story. Sergei had told me the story of his parents' lives and it has stayed with me as one of the most painful and tragic stories I have ever heard, in the same sense as the story of our Holocaust survivor relatives, Ada and Shmerl, or my parents.

Yakov Okun was born in the beginning of the 20th century in the city of Krivoi Rog in the Ukraine. He had two sisters and very poor parents who tried their best to make ends meet. At age fifteen or sixteen, Yakov and a few friends from the same neighborhood decided to walk to Eretz Israel and to help to build Palestine (the country of Israel did not yet exist at this time). It was a long and very difficult journey, but they eventually reached their destination, being young, strong, and determined.

The situation in Palestine was treacherous, and the living conditions were intolerable. Malaria and other diseases were spreading among the small population rapidly. But they were *Halutzim* — pioneers with Zionist ideas in their heads. They were ready to put their lives on the line to build their own country.

Yakov stayed in Israel for about five years and put a great deal of effort into constructing, building and paving roads and railroads. He even worked

the soil for the future country of Israel. He was a brilliant man with very
little education, but with a strong desire to change the world for the better.

In the 1920's, many different ideas were discussed and pondered among
the young Jewish settlers. They had come out of the pogroms in Russia and
Poland, where they had experienced hate and inequality. A bleak future was
ahead of them in their old countries. They were disillusioned by the reality
of economic despair and religion's premise of trusting God for the betterment of their lives. They were dreaming about a "Just Society" with social
justice for all people, wanting to establish one form of Utopia or another.
They believed that when Utopia exists, all ethnic differences would disappear. And for that they were ready to fight. Those young intellectuals were
inspired by the ideas of Marx and Lenin, revolution in Russia, and the
promise of a great future. They came to Israel with the cherished aspirations to build a country of their own, to become a nation among other
nations. They were Bolsheviks at heart, and had unstoppable enthusiasm,
idealism and romanticism. The reality of Palestine wasn't so romantic,
though, and after few years, Yakov started dreaming about moving to
France, where he would have the opportunity for a better education and
more active participation in the communist movement. His friends were
not as ambitious as he was or were more Zionist at heart, and stayed in
Palestine to the better end, as it turned out.

Many years later, Sergei and I went to see a high official in *Histadrut*,
the Israeli trade union organization, with some unsolvable bureaucratic
problem. The first thing this high official asked Sergei was, "Are you by any
chance the son of Yakov Okun from Ukraine?" We were shocked by the
coincidence, and our conversation with a lost friend of Sergei's father took
a very unexpected turn. He briefly told us his story, but mostly wanted to
know what had happened to his very good friend from a very, very long
time ago. As I was looking and listening to this man, I could not stop
thinking about how strange life is. We all make our decisions as we choose
our path and our decisions affect not only ourselves, but generations far
into the future. We are all part of a huge puzzle in the making, and one

person can not only change the lives of so many others, but can change the whole puzzle. Those two f riends c hoses uchv ery different lives.

∞

Yakov came to Paris in the early 1920's. His goal was to get the best education possible, and he entered the University of Sorbonne, which was one of the best universities in the world. He had the best years of his life there and got an excellent education, of course. It was a completely new world for him compared to the province in Russia or the life of a hard-working *Halutz* in Palestine.

The 1920's in Paris was a golden age of glamour, elegance, and extravagance. Paris became a worldwide mecca for the artistic avant-garde, and the capital for free-thinking intellectuals. This beautiful city had a magical allure. Paris was alive. The open-air cafés had exquisite cuisine and wines. There were many different concerts performed by famous entertainers, as well as many very popular jazz clubs all over the city. Surrealism flourished, and art galleries attracted a lot of attention. For a young, handsome, and bright Jewish man with a great intellectual capacity, Paris was the place to be.

He integrated into the French society with ease, started to speak perfect French and made many friends. Yakov did not forget his political aspirations, and became part of a group led by very popular French communists. He was very active in the movement and was excited to hear all the great news from Russia about the successes of the Soviet revolution. Trotsky was one of his heroes. Yakov liked the disputes and arguments, the struggles between different ideas, and the discussion of new solutions to world problems. He read a great deal of propaganda and indoctrination in newspapers and books, and believed in a bright future for communism not only in Russia, but eventually all over the world.

In 1928 he met a beautiful 22-year-old Jewish Parisian girl who was working in the fashion industry. Paris was the fashion capital of the world. Tosca Brod was a dream come true for Yakov. She was lighthearted, intelligent, sweet, and kind. They fell in love, got married, and were planning to live happily ever after. Her beloved brother Yanek and his wife Simone approved of Tosca's choice, and they became a very close family. The two young couples worked hard, had nice apartments in Paris and had plenty of money to spend on their bohemian life style.

There was only one subject that they absolutely disagreed on, and often argued about. Yakov had left Russia a long, long time ago and he hadn't seen his parents and sisters during all that time. He wanted to go home for a visit and introduce his young wife to his family. Tosca had no desire to join him for this trip. Being a woman and more of a pragmatist than Yakov, she saw things differently.

"Yakov, what is the matter with you? Don't you read the newspapers and understand that it is a very bad situation in the Ukraine, where your family is? People are suffering! There is not enough food, everyone is poor and who knows what else is happening there?"

"Tosenka, my dear, you read the wrong newspapers. It is all just anti-communist propaganda. Please, don't trust those awful words. Communism is the best system for the people. It gives them equality and prosperity. Trust me, I read a lot. I truly believe that only fifteen years after the revolution, life is good in Russia. Please, let's go for just two weeks, and you'll see it all with your own eyes."

It took Yakov more than two years to convince his wife to join him on this trip to Hell.

The day before the departure Tosca and Yakov invited a big group of friends and family to a goodbye party at one of the best restaurants in Paris. Many years later my mother-in-law would describe this evening to me with many details, recalling the event with unbearable sadness and nostalgia. There were plenty of her favorite appetizers, the best French dinner menu with the best wine, the best fruits and desserts and surely the best French cheese. She could not forgive herself that she did not eat much that evening and told me that she was a very spoiled French girl. That was the last time she and Yakov saw and ate real food.

CHAPTER TWENTY-ONE

With a heavy heart and with recognition of a real tragedy, I reflect on the next episode of their lives.

It was the summer of 1932 when, after saying goodbye to the family, they boarded the train to Ukraine and arrived in the midst of one of the worst famines ever recorded in the history of the world. It was a manmade disaster, brought about by Stalin's goal of liquidation of private property owned by the *kulaks* (farmers') households in areas where collectivization was being implemented. The entire peasant population that resisted the new brutal changes was wiped out. *Kulaks* were blamed for the absence of the food. They were a class enemy and deserved to die.

The other important goal of Stalin's was to destroy the human spirit. He and his comrades succeeded in both. It was the war of Moscow against the Ukrainian people and the other republics, with the goal of Russification of the U.S.S.R. From this time on there would be only one central government for all, and Moscow would have unlimited power over the whole empire and its people.

By the summer of 1932, millions of people had starved to death and the regime had strategically murdered many of its people. When Tosca would tell me her stories about this period of her life, I always thought that she was exaggerating, perhaps going a little overboard. Even though I had heard the horror stories of the Siege of Leningrad during the war, it was hard to believe the level of atrocities and crimes of Stalin's regime on its *own* people in the time of *peace*. Ukraine was always considered to be the best agricultural part of the land, "black-earth," the bread-basket of Czarist Russia.

Soviets, after Stalin's death, admitted to a lot of "mistakes" in their tactics in reaching their goals, as I remember, but refused to recognize the famine in Ukraine for the disaster that it really was. They always proclaimed that everything was done for the glorious future of the U.S.S.R. and that all means would be justified in reaching this goal.

I could not understand back then why the European and American journalists who were visiting Russia did not give this information to the world. How could Yakov and Tosca be absolutely fooled, living in Paris? I think some journalists were great sympathizers for the cause. Easily manipulated by the Soviets, they were either deceived or deceiving, and they were given Potemkin-like tours of only prepared, dedicated areas. No one wanted to believe those few reports about the famine that Tosca referred to in her conversations with Yakov in Paris.

This young Parisian couple, expensively and fashionably dressed, came to visit the family in the midst of that disaster. Tosca understood the situation right away and was counting the days until her departure to return back home. She was horrified and hated every moment of seeing what was happening around her. They had brought some cans of food with them, just in case. She described to me how alarmed she was when they would throw away the garbage after finishing a meal. They would see and hear screaming children running toward the dumpsters, and fighting over the empty cans. Just the smell of the food would make them delirious. Yakov asked Tosca to come to the bread store with him. As they were waiting in the very long line, Tosca told him that everybody had some kind of cards. His answer was,

"We'll just give them some cash. Relax, Tosenka, the situation is not that bad."

But there was no bread without those special cards, and they had to leave the store empty-handed.

I can only imagine their frustration, disappointment, and regret about this journey, which was supposed to have been a great, welcoming trip home. Tosca probably said, "I told you so!" a few times. I know I would have. But she was a very polite girl, and she knew that they would be leaving this horrible nightmare in a couple of days. Maybe she let this pass in hopes that he would learn his lessons and would be ready to listen to her opinion more carefully in the future. There was another emotional separation with the family before they headed to the train station, but Tosca was counting the minutes until her departure for Paris and would never look back.

They were stopped at the gate, after showing their papers and passports. They were told unequivocally that under some provision of the Soviet government, they could not leave the country and would have to follow the officer to a special room for further instructions. Tosca panicked right away, feeling the unexpected turn of events as the scary harbinger of a horrific future. Yakov believed that it was just a misunderstanding, and the higher authority would let them get on the train and go to Paris right after he explained that they never intended to stay in Russia. After all, Tosca was not a Soviet citizen and he had a French passport. But nothing helped, and they were told to leave the premises of the train station immediately. They were promised to get some kind of explanation later.

For Tosca it was like a death sentence, a crash of her life, the dead end of the road, an unbearable tragedy. She was in complete panic and disarray, trembling in fear; *Why did they stop us? What did we do wrong? What kind of country is this, what kind of laws do they have? I just want to go home; I do not want to be here even one more day! Why are they so impolite and did not even want to talk to us? Why are they so inconsiderate and cruel?* She thought that unfortunately, she did not speak Russian; otherwise, she would be more persuasive in convincing the authorities than Yakov. She refused to leave the station. She sobbed uncontrollably. She begged in French. She felt nauseated, almost fainting, feeling deprived of her rights as a French citizen. For the first time in her life she felt humiliated, powerless and discarded. Cold fear stabbed her right through her heart and made the fire within her burn. An obnoxious officer with ugly smirk on his face had no patience for this entire dramatic scene and told Yakov to get her the hell out of there immediately. Otherwise, both of them would be arrested on the spot and go to jail.

Poor Tosca! My heart always goes out to her, more so than to Yakov. She was just an innocent bystander, a wife who was trying to please her husband. How would she understand at this moment that her fate, her destiny had just crossed paths with one of the most inhumane, atrocious, brutal, deadly and criminal regimes known in history? This was the beginning of the era of Stalin's most painful acts of brutality against his people, the evil march against the so-called counter-revolutionary activities, the purification and reeducation of the masses. Stalin's Gulag was on the horizon.

Yakov and Tosca were waiting in vain for permission to leave, while they were starving with everyone else. They went to all the authorities with the request to leave, and they were refused without a real explanation.

Life took a different path from that point, and they both had to make adjustments. Tosca wrote to her brother Yanek, and was waiting for his response. She did not know one word in the Russian language and was forced to start learning this foreign tongue. Yakov was looking for a different place to go, far away from Ukraine. They moved to a small city near Moscow, after he found a job as a bookkeeper. In the new place, they continued to beg authorities for permission to leave and go back to Paris, but with every passing year, it became clearer that this would never happen.

People often seem to be able to bring themselves out of despair by their strong drive to survive and perpetuate. A few years later, Yakov and Tosca had a sweet little son, and they named him the typical Russian name Sergei, with the nickname of Serioja or, the sweet version, Seriojenka. What a great decision it would be for my life, even though I was not in the picture for the next thirty years. But I love my in-laws for bringing my beloved husband into this world.

As the couple began to lose hope in the possibility of ever returning to Paris, they began to build their new Soviet life. They thought that with time everything would be straightened out and eventually, they would get the permission to leave. How naïve they were, how little they understood about the tragic future developments that would bring everyone to their knees and make Tosca's life a tragedy of Shakespearean proportions.

CHAPTER TWENTY-TWO

Soviet officials came to arrest Yakov in the middle of the night on the charges of espionage and connection with some counter-revolutionary organization abroad. The absurdity of this accusation did not matter. He disappeared, and Tosca had no idea where he was and when or if he would be coming back. She went from one office to another, inquiring about her husband to no avail. I am sure she shed a lot of tears during those long sleepless nights, feeling desperate, lost, tragically sad, and bewildered. But in the morning she also felt the strong responsibility of motherhood and understood that there was no time to feel sorry for herself. Her little son had to survive. She found some job to make a little money, her Russian became much better, and she put all her energy into raising her child.

They did not see Yakov for a few years, and then suddenly, he was released as unexpectedly as he had disappeared. Yakov did not tell her much about prison but believed that it was just a misunderstanding, and life would now be back to normal. I do not remember what Tosca told me about the wartime, except that they had another son in 1945 and called him Victor, for the victory in the war. She did not have any information about her family in Paris, and only many years later heard the stories of their survival in France. Her extended family in Poland had perished in Hitler's concentration camps.

The last part of their story overtook them like a runaway train. Right after the victory in the war with Hitler, Stalin's plan to finish the unfinished war against the Enemies of the People was fueled with more energy and strength. Yakov was arrested again, but this time on charges that were both more serious and more bogus. He was interrogated and tortured to get some kind of confession before they sentenced him to ten years of corrective forced labor camp and sent him to one of the most deadly and notorious camps: Magadan in Northeast Siberia.

Millions had worked and died in those labor camps. A 12 to16-hour work day in the gold mines, starvation diet, inadequate clothing in the minus 50-degree brutal winter — this was the extreme punishment for millions of people, most of whom had no idea why they were brought there to die. Magadan was the worst of these slave camps, one of the most severe and sadistic in the world.

This time, Tosca was informed that her husband was an "Enemy of the People" and, like many others, he had been sent to Magadan. She had no family in Russia except for Yakov and her two sons, so she decided to move to Magadan to be close to her husband, even though she would never see him there. It was an extremely difficult life, but she survived it all and raised two great human beings. It is a triumph of the human spirit that astonishes me. Many years later, Tosca would tell me a few stories about the time in Magadan. She had the most adorable French accent that was music to my ears, but her stories were horrifying to hear.

At age 11 or 12 Sergei, who was probably bored to death in his classroom, learning the history of the Communist Party, doodled a little picture in his textbook of Lenin and Stalin playing soccer. He used the two little photos in the book. This innocent picture, when seen by the teacher, was reported to the authorities and an arrest warrant was issued right away for Sergei, the Enemy's son. He was accused of a full range of anti-political activities and disrespect for the Holiest of Holy Leader and Commander of the U.S.S.R., Iosif Stalin. They were ready to send Sergei to the children's camp and Tosca knew right away that she would lose not only her husband, but also her son, who understandably was her life.

She was out of her mind with fear and anger, and putting her own life on the line, she went to war against the authorities with all her might. She was running from one office to another, begging for understanding, explaining that her son did not mean any disrespect, that he is just a child. She was crying and pleading, literally falling on her knees before these ruthless bureaucrats. She begged for their mercy, but nobody wanted to take a chance and accommodate her. It was dangerous for them to go against the flow, and nobody seemed to care.

But luckily, she came across one officer who probably had some humanity left in him. Maybe he also had a son at home. He made a decision, against all odds, to cancel the warrant and put his signature on it. Tosca couldn't hide her tears telling me this story. She had such a heartfelt appreciation to her unsung hero.

In one respect my mother-in-law was extremely lucky. They never arrested her for simply being the wife of an Enemy of the People, or for being a foreigner. Thousands of innocent women were sent to these camps, leaving their children behind in the orphanages. Stalin's plan was to raise a new generation of communists that would forget their roots, and forget their parents. Their first attachment must be to the Communist Party, then to the Homeland. Many children who were raised in those orphanages did not even know whether their parents had been executed or were still alive. And at some point, they almost forgot that they had ever had mothers and fathers.

It took three years after Stalin's death in 1953, for Yakov to finally come back to his family, more than two decades after his departure from Paris in 1932. What a tragically broken life, full of broken dreams, and broken humanity. Instead of the life of joy and fulfillment they had hoped for, Yakov and Tosca spent their lives facing Evil and Terror. Yakov went to the corrective labor camp as a young, healthy man and came back home old, sick and very weak.

The slave labor camps had taken their toll on him. He passed away just a few years later, but to the end of his days, he never lost the belief that the ideas of his youth were still great ideas, and it was just the implementation that went horribly wrong.

CHAPTER TWENTY-THREE

Yakov brought Tosca from Heaven to Hell, but his son, Sergei brought me, his wife, out of Hell to Heaven.

The several years after the *ulpan* in Israel, as I mentioned, were the best years of my life and the life of our whole family. The small occurrences in life that people enjoy as normal were very new to us. We loved our new apartment. Never before had we experienced such unbelievable luxury. For the first time in our lives, we would go to little shops to buy tasty fruits and vegetables, even in the wintertime. In Russia we never had fresh fruits or vegetables during winters, only for a couple of months in the summer. The variety of different foods, the assortment, the aroma, the unfamiliar delicacies, the politeness of the sales people, the *Shook* (market place) with its middle-eastern flavors, and the abundance of food were astonishing for us.

Sergei would go to work in the morning, and I would enjoy setting up the apartment in expectation of our new baby, cooking the best meals I knew how, bringing Anechka to the newly built preschool and feeling so beautiful in all my new bright pregnancy clothes, blending in with the other pregnant Israeli women, pretending that I was one of them. Anechka's teacher suggested to me that we change our daughter's name once again.

"Hanna is a very old fashioned name for a little girl," she said. "Please, change it to Anat. This is a name from the Torah. Your daughter is such a beautiful girl, and the new name will fit her better."

Sergei agreed, and that is how Anya/Anechka/Annushka/Hanna became known as Anat from that time forward.

I remember smiling most of the time and drinking from this well of happiness that I had never experienced before. There is no higher pleasure in life than when you have just a simple peace in your entire being and are breathing the air of freedom while living your unrestricted simple life. I listened to my husband and went to Heaven on Earth. What a tremendous difference from the story of Yakov and Tosca!

I felt so blessed and so calm, just waiting for Sergei to come home from work and enjoy a nice dinner together. Little everyday blissful moments, the joy of having your beloved with you and building a new life, expecting a child. We would go to Tivon to see my family. What great trips we had into the beautiful countryside, and what pure joy there was in seeing everyone happy!

My parents' Yiddish came alive, the language of their childhood, their *mamaloshen*. They met a few people their age and befriended them. In many ways it was easier for my parents to adjust to the local culture, than it was for us. Jewish music, all those Yiddish songs and dances, and Yiddish theater brought back so much happiness for my Mama and Papa. I was really surprised myself, when here and there I understood such a familiar, but completely forgotten, tongue. An "Aha!" moment for me:

"That was the language that I had heard so many years ago from my Babushka!"

Suddenly, the memory of my Babushka, that had faded away for a long time came back to me and would stay with me forever.

Some of my mother's habits began to change; like she would stop doing certain things on Shabbat.

"What is that, Mama, why?" I would ask in complete surprise.

"We should not work or continue our normal activities on this special day," my Mama would explain to me. I had never heard any of this all through my life. They would have a nice *Kabbalat-Shabbat*, the greeting for Shabbat services that would include prayers, songs and a special delicious dinner in their *ulpan*. My parents would feel at home with all these rituals, which were unknown to us. Apparently, they knew a lot of those Jewish customs and were familiar with all the holidays. I only remembered a few Yiddish songs from my childhood that my father liked to sing. Otherwise, Sergei and I had to start from the beginning, taking baby steps into this new world of anything Jewish, whereby my parents easily continued from where they had left off many years ago. I loved seeing my parents rejoicing again after all those years of suffering.

The owner of their *ulpan* was a Polish gentleman, a Holocaust survivor. His whole attitude toward newcomers was so much more welcoming and kind than anything that we experienced in our *ulpan*. He had a unique positive energy and spent a lot of time with my parents and the rest of the emigrants, being always very positive and supportive in their new journey to the new life. It was not an easy transition and many of his residents needed and appreciated his guidance. Thank you, God, for all those blessings to my parents, even though they had to wait many years to receive them. Sergei and I attended a couple of those *Kabbalat-Shabbats* in their *ulpan* and we were surprised by the unexpected beauty of the unknown rituals, lighting the candles, soulful melodies of the prayers, and peacefulness of the moment.

So, while still in the *ulpan*, Sergei and I decided to check out a local synagogue for Shabbat services. Except for the Leningrad experience during *Simhat-Torah*, we had never set foot inside a synagogue. This turned out to be a strange and even bizarre endeavor for us.

As we opened the door of one of the local small orthodox synagogues, we saw many men moving in a ritualistic back and forth motion, with their heads moving up and down in some hidden rhythm. They were all bearded men, and there were no women in sight. They were dressed in some kind of very old-fashioned black suits, covered with white shawls and chanting unfamiliar melodies. No one paid any attention to us. They saw us standing at the entrance door, but did not welcome or greet us. We stood there for a while in amazement and curiosity, but felt very uncomfortable, out of place and uninvited.

We felt like intruders into somebody else's party, not belonging to this awkward world of some bizarre group of men. It was a very disappointing introduction into the real Jewish religious life, and it stopped us from being interested. But Shmerl told us that when our son would be born we would have to conduct *Brit-Milah* (*Bris*), or circumcision, according to *Halahah* – Jewish law, whatever that meant. I was apprehensive about the whole project, but Sergei assured me that he would figure it all out, and told me not to worry. Later I understood that a *Bris* meant the covenant between the Jewish People and God.

CHAPTER TWENTY-FOUR

My father decided to look for some relatives from his side of the family who supposedly lived in Israel. My Babushka Malka — my father's mother — had three brothers of the Korobochko family, who had left Russia for South Africa when they all were very young. She wanted to go too, and received all the necessary papers from her brothers to follow their footsteps. They were ready to leave Russia when suddenly her husband, my Dedushka Nohem, got a raise of one ruble at his job and decided to stay, refusing to make a drastic change to their penniless existence.

Poor Malka! She was a bright and intelligent woman, and had a clear understanding of the upcoming tragic events in her life and in the life of the country that she did not want to be a part of. With all her logic she tried very hard to convince her stubborn husband to change his mind. After a lot of pleading, tears and anger she had to give up and to succumb to her husband's unwillingness to make a bold decision.

Malka regretted this decision all her life. I do not think they were a compatible couple and I never thought that they had a loving or happy relationship. Dedushka Nohem just was not an adventurous, clever or worldly man. I remember him being kind of gloomy, un-cheerful and un-playful. He had little interest in my sister or me. He also had a severe form of diabetes and had his legs amputated. So, I remember him being glued to his chair during the last years of his life. Wheelchairs were not provided to elderly invalids of his stature. So, he attached little wheels to his chair and in this way, Malka was able to push and to move the chair a little bit around the room and to the restroom, down the long corridor. My father's sister Maya, her husband, and their daughter shared one small room with my grandparents. The communal apartment had six or seven families living in it, sharing one kitchen and one restroom with no shower. What a tragic ending to Malka's dream life!

There was only one lasting thing my grandfather passed down to us —
the Guretzky family name.

My father was much closer to his mother than to his father. I always felt
a deep connection and strong bond between them. Babushka Malka always
looked at my father with proud eyes and a lot of love. He showed her a
lot of respect and liked to share his problems with her with admiration for
her wisdom and problem solving abilities. I remember thinking even as a
child that they had some inner understanding of each other without many
words, as only mother and son can have. I do not think that my mother
necessarily liked this closeness too much, feeling maybe that he was a bit
of a "Mama's boy," but I enjoyed the unspoken tie my father had with his
Mama. I don't know why, but I remember Babushka Malka often ironically
and regretfully called her four sons "my Americans." They were a tall and
handsome bunch, and I imagined how unfortunate she must have felt to
have to raise them in the *shtetl* of Mozir, Belorussia, instead of America or
South Africa.

Sometime during the summer of 1964, a couple of her South African
brothers with their wives, unexpectedly for me, came to visit Malka in
Leningrad. It was a fascinating experience for all of us. Apparently, she
had never stopped her brave communications with them through the mail
service, even during the worst times of Stalin's Russia. Malka, like her
brother Simon, had guts and decided to continue writing letters to them no
matter what. Somehow, a few activities in Russia were not always punished
and officials allowed this correspondence to exist, against all logic. This
never made sense to me, but I guess some things would always fall through
the cracks, no matter what. It was just impossible to imprison more than
250 million people in the Soviet Union.

To me, those South Africans were like aliens who came to earth from
a different planet. They looked and were dressed like aliens — handsome
aliens, to be sure. Their manners were like aliens, yet they spoke Yiddish
with Babushka Malka, which, unfortunately, I couldn't understand.

They were such a happy, smiley and talkative people, the likes of which
I had never seen before. They looked very, very rich, like those foreign

"capitalists" who we were conditioned to hate, those exploiters of the working class. But they seemed to be very nice and sweet people! Still, I felt most uncomfortable, inadequate and provincial in their company. The contrast between us was staggering and very painful. What a tremendous difference our birthplace can make in our lives! How breathtakingly lucky all those relatives were just by the virtue of making the right decisions in their life! I just thought that Babushka Malka must have been so embarrassed to host them in the poverty in which she lived. She probably was feeling awful that she had listened to her weak husband and did not follow her ambitious heart and her successful brothers. She must have felt like such a failure, and hated her husband for their family's horrible lives. I felt really compassionate toward her, but did not know what to say or do about it. Those seemingly simple or difficult decisions that we make can turn our lives upside down and sometimes cause tragic consequences.

To our surprise, Papa found the family of his second cousin from South Africa in the *kibbutz* Shluhot near Beit-Shean in the northeast of Israel. Menucha, a daughter of one of Malka's brothers, and her husband Eliezer invited us to come for a visit. We were very happy and excited to get out of the *ulpan* and meet this real Israeli family of ours. At the same time we had very little understanding about *kibbitzum*. It seemed to us like some communist communal living that we did not care for at all. With mixed feelings, uncertainty and curiosity we took our first long trip by the bus to Beit-Shean.

The religious kibbutz Shluhot was established by the youth of one of the Jewish organizations from South Africa and was a very successful and happy place to be. We loved every moment of this place right away, and loved Menucha and Eliezer with their special charm that most South Africans have (and the rest of us do not). Even now, I find that most South Africans are a little different and a unique breed of Jews! We loved their five sons too, and we were fascinated about everything in and about the kibbutz — their life style, their communal living and working, children raised separately from their parents, their huge *Hadar-Ohel* (dining hall), where everyone can eat an abundant variety of the tasteful, fresh, organic, home-grown food.

Mostly, we were fascinated by their religious rituals. During Shabbat service, the first floor of the beautiful building was full of men without the long beards and black suits, who were dressed in white shirts instead. Women, as in the first synagogue, were not seen, but I discovered them on the second floor. That was a fascinating experience for all of us, but Sergei and I couldn't yet make up our mind about all this new information concerning Judaism. Our impression of the kibbutz synagogue was very different form our impression of the first synagogue we experienced in Haifa, much more pleasant. Here we saw a younger and older crowd together in an uplifting and even happy mood, very welcoming fellowship, and a joyful choir singing the prayers with the rhythmical movement of their bodies. People felt free to walk around, talking, smiling, hugging, and greeting each other. *Shabbat Shalom* was expressed by everyone. Many children were dressed very nicely especially for Shabbat, participating in children's services.

Menucha explained to us that there are certain rules that must be followed: men and women were separated for a reason, and men couldn't shake hands or give a hug to any women, except their wives. We did not understand the reasons, and our language barrier did not allow us to explore more. But the atmosphere of the Shabbat was joyful, celebratory, with special candle lighting and a lot of songs and prayers for Shabbat. The communal dinner was a unique experience with the friendliest families and a lot of children enjoying a delicious meal together with energy of contentment and peacefulness.

As strange as it was, Sergei and I admitted to each other that apparently Israelis created an unusual positive experience of living together on the principle of equality and being able to share everything with each other without discomfort or hard feelings. It was unimaginable for us, coming from the Soviet Union. But the idyllic setting survived only for couple of generations before it started to decline and needed a fundamental restructure. We had the feeling that the great ideas of equality cannot be sustained for a long time anyway. It seems to be against human nature. But we were surprised that it worked even for as long as it did. Only in Israel!

We became very close with Menucha's family and tried to visit them as often as we could. And I should not neglect to mention the unreal natural beauty of this place, nested in the foothills of the Gilboa Mountains in the Spring Valley, with amazing scenery, spectacular landscape, with different types of palm trees, the bluest sky, and dry air. It was a real paradise.

CHAPTER TWENTY-FIVE

As the day of our son's birth was getting closer, we started to get nervous about the arrival of Sergei's mother, Tosca, and his brother Victor. They were on their way to Israel from Russia, after finally getting permission to join the family and be on time for the birth of our son, a new Yakov Okun. We wanted to give Tosca this happy moment, to witness a revival of her legacy, to show her a glimpse of a better future.

My whole pregnancy was a pure joy with unbelievable doctors' care, exercise programs and great nutrition.

My first pregnancy with Anat in Russia was so different, so much more difficult. We had to stand in endless lines to get any food. During the first six months in the cold wintery weather, there was no variety of fruits or vegetables. The majority of our diet was poor quality frozen chicken, bread and carrots, cabbage and potatoes. Papa would stand in line after work for a limited amount of oranges imported from abroad and whatever else might be sold during the evening in the stands outside of the stores in freezing weather. The stores didn't have enough room for those long lines, so they would open those stands outside. People would not even ask what was for sale. They would go straight to the end of the line to wait, hoping to get some of whatever was being offered. Everything was a *shortage*, scarce and very hard to find.

During my pregnancy, I was also terrified to walk outside and possibly fall down on the slippery snowy streets or to use the overcrowded public transportation. To buy anything for the baby was a challenge and a big problem. It took Sergei months to find a baby tub, made out of some kind of heavy metal, which weighed a ton. Medical care was also lousy, and I was just worried about the whole process. Our happiness of having our first baby was not in sync with our miserable surroundings.

The whole process of delivering babies in Russia was a nightmare. I had a hospital in mind for the delivery, the same one where my sister had been born many years prior. When I was ready for delivery at two o'clock in the morning, Sergei called the taxi, and Mama, Sergei and I were on our way. The taxi dropped us off by the hospital, and as we walked toward the entrance, we noticed that the whole hospital was absolutely dark. Alarmed and anxious, we read a little note on the door stating to our dismay that for whatever reason the hospital was closed for the next few days. It was September 30th and didn't begin to compare with what my Mama went through during the dead of winter when I was born. Nevertheless, there were no taxis, or cars for that matter, driving on the streets of Leningrad at three o'clock in the morning. I didn't know whether to laugh or to cry, but the prospect of delivering the baby on the street with Sergei's and Mama's help was the last thing on my wish list.

We stood on the street, in hopes that maybe at least one car would appear by pure magic. And after a while, when I was already in a real panic, we saw a car and Sergei jumped into the middle of the street to prevent this car from driving by. The car stopped and all three of us were begging the passenger of this lone taxi to let us in, considering the situation, and drive us to a different hospital. He was not happy about the interruption of his trip and our unexpected intrusion, but I probably was begging him so passionately, looked so pregnant, so big, and so needy that finally he had mercy on me. Sergei helped to push me into this small car and the taxi driver drove us to the hospital.

I entered the huge labor room, filled with about thirty screaming ladies. The nurse told me to lie down on a hard bed and wait for the doctor. Nobody came for a long time and I was just scared to death. I was surrounded by screaming women, and rude nurses were shouting at them,

"Shut up, it's not your time yet. Stop yelling like mad; stop your hysteria, shut up!"

Obviously, there was no epidural or any other pain relievers available, and the negligence from uncaring medical professionals was horrific.

I was very quiet, trying not to anger anybody. A nurse came and finally checked on me and gave some shot of whatever she decided was right for me, since my water had broken a long time ago. When my pain became absolutely unbearable and I raised my voice, the nurse came to check and started screaming at me.

"Are you crazy? The baby is coming and you're lying here without a scream? How in the hell should I know that you are ready?"

They rushed me to a delivery room, while I was thinking about what my mom was screaming as she was giving birth to me. And then I stopped thinking altogether for a while, and my daughter was born shortly after that. They transferred me to a different huge room with many, many beds, where all the new mothers were recovering from their brutal birth experiences. It was impossible to rest. Now it was the babies who were screaming, and they were bringing them in to be nursed.

I didn't see my daughter for the next three days. They told me that because the umbilical cord was around her neck during birth, she wasn't ready to be brought to me and to be nursed. No further explanation was given to me or to Sergei. He would come to the hospital every day during the whole week to bring me some food from home. Men were not allowed into the hospitals at that time. In any weather they would stand outside of the hospital and shout their wife's name to the closed windows in hope of getting a glimpse of their wives or maybe even their newborn babies.

When finally they brought Anechka to me for the first time, I recognized her immediately among the thirty plus babies lying on the huge moving platform. She was the most beautiful baby in the whole world with her long black hair and blue eyes. I loved her from this very moment and forever.

As terrible as this experience was for me, it was even worse for my sister one year later. After giving birth to her first child, the doctors forgot about her in the delivery room. She was bleeding, but nobody was around and nobody came for the next few hours, leaving her bleeding to death.

After a few hours, a cleaning lady came into the room and saw Lala lying there unattended.

"What in the hell is going on? *Boje moi*, my God, what a mess, lady," she pronounced angrily. "Blood is everywhere! Are you still alive in there?" That fortunate moment allowed my sister to survive.

This was not such an unusual situation in Soviet hospitals. Nobody really cared. The gynecologists were mostly busy performing endless abortions, since this was the only birth control method available in the great U.S.S.R. Women would often have more than ten abortions during the best years of their lives. The hospital workers were understaffed and underpaid. There was no motivation for better service, no desire for innovation, no responsibility, and no kindness. It was just hard work from morning till night and then going home to miserable living conditions, earning small salaries that provided them a very low standard of living. A doctor's profession was never considered prestigious in the U.S.S.R., and most of the doctors were tired, overworked women.

CHAPTER TWENTY-SIX

I gave birth to my son in Heaven, compared to my Russian experience. A beautiful clean hospital with personal attention to all my needs and wants, rooms for just a few women, doctors and nurses who treated me like a princess, kind and patient responses to my requests, attentiveness and smiling faces, bringing me water when I am thirsty or giving me great food, even if I am not really hungry, doctors who are monitoring my progress and giving me the explanation of what is going on and what is the next step, the tender touch of nurses, holding my hand when necessary. Husbands were still not allowed to be with their wives during the birth, but right after the birth they were allowed to come for a visit and stay as long as they wanted. No wonder that Israeli women often had many children!!

Finally, when I heard my baby's scream and it was over, the doctor asked me:

"Who do you have at home, Geveret Okun? A daughter? Well, Mazel Tov, now you have a beautiful son, a *sabra* (native Israeli)," and she showed me Yakov and put him on my chest and I was in Heaven with tears of blissful happiness from this moment and forever. I was only surprised that he had no resemblance to Anechka and had very long, blond patches of hair. Joyful Sergei and my Mama came soon after with a colorful bouquet of flowers, surprised at what an unexpectedly short time it took and how great I looked. And then they met Yakov for the first time and Sergei's heart just melted from the unbearably overwhelming happiness.

As we were preparing for the day of *Brit-Milah* we received the information, that by a pure miracle, not a coincidence, Tosca was on her way to Israel, but we had to wait a couple of days. Shmerl was discussing the situation with the Rabbi to get permission to postpone the *Bris*, which by Jewish law has to be on the eighth day after the birth. Considering the unusual circumstances, we were able to postpone it until their arrival a couple of days later. Finally, Tosca and Victor entered our apartment and the reunion of our whole family was magical.

That was a most unusual day in our lives. The whole family was together. Everybody was so excited and happy, hugs and kisses all around, Eliezer was smiling contentedly. Everybody was congratulating Sergei, who was absolutely overexcited and overwhelmed. For the first time in several generations, we were allowed to participate in and were ready for a Jewish ritual in our own family. *Wow!!* Anat was kissed and hugged by everybody, but mostly by Baba Tosca; colored pictures were taken. And finally Shmerl took his position, and an old Rabbi with a very long grey beard was ready to begin.

I was very nervous, and didn't understand what exactly to expect. I brought my treasured boy and put him onto the pillow on Shmerl's lap, honoring this Hero of mine, as promised. The chanting began and the voice of the Rabbi brought out so many of my hidden emotions, coming through the past generations to the present generation, broken for a while, but still alive, unexpected, but almost a familiar feeling of belonging to some magical moment of a Jewish covenant, of the presence of the unknown to me God of Abraham, Isaac and Jacob, belonging to something bigger than me and my family.

Suddenly, I was part of *My People*, yes, of *My People*, whose fate is my fate, whose past is my past, whose history is my history, whose suffering is my suffering, whose prayers are my prayers, whose music is my music, whose rituals are my rituals, and whose God is my God. I felt it with all my heart and all my soul, even though I was not ready yet to admit it. I felt that I was in a trance, and then suddenly I heard our son crying. I took him into my arms. Sergei, more emotional than I had ever seen him before, was hugging Anechka and me, and everybody was lifting their wine glasses

"*L'chaim!* To Life! *L'chaim!*, *Mazel Tov!*, *Mazel Tov!*, Congratulations!" Yakov had his first portion of wine, and now was calm and happy.

And my mother was hugging Tosca. Tears of happiness were in their eyes…

Oh, God, preserve this moment, the triumph of our human spirit, our ability to overcome unthinkable tragedies, and stay alive and continue living with all the strength and love, that you, God, are giving us….I am forever grateful…

CHAPTER TWENTY-SEVEN

Our blissful life continued uninterrupted for the next few years. For his first birthday Yashenka received a great present — his cousin Avi was born and my sister Lala and Mark had their own big celebration of *Brit-Milah* for their baby boy according to *Halahah*. We were not allowed to perform this simple ritual of circumcision in the U.S.S.R, and Misha, their older son, had to undergo the procedure in the hospital in Israel at age four — poor Michael!

It was an unbelievably happy childhood for our children. We moved to our own new apartments in Kiryat-Yam near Haifa, ten minutes away from the beaches of the Mediterranean Sea. We lived in the same building as Lala and Mark, and my parents' apartment was only fifteen minutes walking distance away from us. We were a very close and loving family, helping each other in every way and enjoying every moment of our new life. We started to integrate into Israeli life, started to understand the culture of the new country little by little, and loved Israeli music, songs and dances. We celebrated all the holidays with the help of our older children, who acquired a great deal of information from school. They were becoming truer Israelis by the minute. The children loved to play outside and had many good friends. They had more fun in those few years than my sister or I had ever dreamed about.

All I remember about my childhood and school years is darkness and boredom. We had, literally, no toys to play with and nothing much to do around the apartment. Our parents worked six days a week and would come home late and overtired. Babushka Meita, my mother's Mama, would spend most of the day cooking dinner for everybody, including her younger daughter Ida who lived with us until she got married a few years later. So, it was a long cooking day to prepare even the simplest meal for six people on a little kerosene stove. The rest of the day, Babushka would try to warm up the very cold rooms by attempting to light up the wet, moist and damp pieces of wood in a special round *pechka* (furnace). She would often become frustrated for not being able to succeed. We did not have hot water, shower, or telephone in our tiny apartment. Our clothes were washed in a small washbasin in cold water with a piece of cheap, dark soap. Drying the clothes was also challenging. Babushka tried her best to be a good housekeeper and a babysitter, but she had a limited amount of energy to do all the chores perfectly. Washing dishes and clothes were pushing her limits. There also was no window in the dark kitchen, nor was there any ventilation. There was no fresh air to breathe.

Babushka was very busy all day long, and my sister and I had nothing to do. And so we would run around the table making a lot of noise, laughing and falling down and running again and then toward each other, bumping into each other, and Babushka would worry that one of us could be injured. She would try to stop us, scream at us to stop, but how else could we amuse ourselves during six months of very cold winters in Leningrad?

Many times we would take all the chairs and build a "train" and pretend to travel to faraway places. I would also make up some imaginary stories and make my sister laugh or be scared. Lala still remembers my Oscar-like performances of made-up theatrical scenes of tragedies that I would present for her. I loved doing it, especially seeing her emotional response. I also liked to put on fashion shows for her entertainment, using the very few articles from my mother's clothing. This was the natural expression of my true creative and feminine nature, which was also expressed through my love of dancing and music. Listening to the poor sounding music and Soviet songs or stories on the one accessible radio station was the only entertainment available to us.

Having Babushka around was a blessing for me and also for my mother. At least she didn't have to do all the chores after the long hours of work each day. The warmth and love of my Babushka and my parents compensated for the humdrum existence of my early childhood. And the taste of some Babushka's simple dishes, even though they were so repetitive, has stayed with me all through my life and has been passed down through me to my children, and even my grandchildren.

My awareness of and inner confrontation with Death was thrown onto me unexpectedly at a tender age and wounded me very deeply. I had just entered my first grade in school, Aunt Ida had her first child and Babushka would leave us a few times on Sundays to be with her newborn granddaughter Svetlana.

Babushka was with us that ordinary evening in February of 1951, and life was very normal, as usual. We went to sleep at the normal time, and that night, I woke up and tried to wake up Babushka, for whatever reason. There was no answer, even after a few repetitions of my request. I raised my voice – no answer. That probably had never happened before, so I got up and started to climb onto her bed. And then something absolutely unexpected hit me in the gut with the power of a horrifying reality – I had touched Death — Babushka's cold, dead body.

I can still feel this touch, even now, like it happened yesterday, and I can hear my scream to my mother, through the darkness of the night, not even realizing yet what had really happened and how my life would be impacted by this moment for many years to come.

I see my mother rushing into the room and then my father. She is trying to wake Babushka up, shaking her, talking Yiddish to her, begging her to wake up and realizing that it is the end; hysterical, screaming, wailing, crazy untamed emotions, losing her mind. My sister is awake now and screaming and crying too; my papa is trying to calm my Mama down to no avail.

I am personally witnessing a tragedy of humanity for the first time. I do not know anything about Death. I am absolutely not prepared for this turn of events. I had never seen those raw emotions before and I think, that my Babushka is the only one who has ever died, and that is why my Mama is in this disastrous disarray and out of control, not even paying attention to me, not even saying a word to me, not even explaining to me what just happened.

I feel scared, shaking, and afraid to cry, not wanting to upset Mama even more. I hug my sister and try to calm her down, but seeing my Mama crying out loud, nonstop and saying some Yiddish words out loud and not responding to my father's kind words makes everything seem as though it is just spinning out of control. I blocked out the full development of the next few hours, but I remember my father leaving to make a call from the public telephone booth to my Aunt Fania and after a while I see her appear in our place and she and Mom hug each other and cry together for a long, long time. Later this day my Aunt Ida rushed into the room and all three sisters were crying uncontrollably...

The most upsetting event for me and my sister was my Mama's decision to leave us overnight in my sister's preschool. I vaguely remember that apparently a service like this was available in the U.S.S.R. for children to be left overnight for as many nights as necessary. To be there alone after witnessing this tragic display of unbearable and uncontrolled pain and emotion shook my soul to the core, left me breathless and stayed in my head, my eyes and my ears for life. I never talked about this whole episode with my mother, never complained, and never asked for an explanation of the strange behavior that I had witnessed. I think that my mother was extremely close with Babushka, who was only 63 years old and was not even sick. She died the best possible death, like an angel, during peaceful sleep in her own bed; *Halevai Aleinu* (wishing it upon any of us).

But for my mother, it happened so unexpectedly, so abruptly. After the war, her nervous system was just shot. She could take only so much of life's tragedies and the death of her mother was above her ability to cope. Mama was very weak and was often sick during my childhood. Ambulances would come often to help her with her heart problems and sometimes would take her to the hospital. She would always try to pretend that she was OK, but my father would see through it and would always try to help her. The war left deep scars in my mother's soul, and as strong as she was, the death of her mother probably caused a flood of anxiety that overflowed her entire being.

Maybe it was my childish perspective of the way things were, or perhaps we all just pretended to accept death with little emotions shown, coming to funerals all dressed up and even smiling, seeing our relatives for the first time in a long time. Maybe each one of us wants to scream and rebel against the reality of the way God created us and the world. We have to say goodbye to our dear ones and continue living like nothing happened, or keep our emotions inside while everybody around us is giving us suggestions and condolences, like it makes a real difference. But everyone is in the same boat of coming to a place of so-called acceptance. Many are trying to believe in the afterlife, but nobody, nobody is sure or knows, and in the meantime, our loved ones are gone and forever gone from our life on earth. The axe of death is always over our heads and heads of our loved ones in so many unexpected ways and we continue living with tears and smiles, and thanking God for our blessings.

Life went on without Babushka, and I had a very cold spot inside of me that I tried to hide. Now suddenly in my mind, everybody around me became vulnerable, mostly my mother. I was afraid to go to sleep and lose my mother during the night. *Babushka was much healthier than my mother,* I thought, *And now any day my Mama would be dead too and leave me behind.* I began the ritual of asking Mom if she was feeling okay every night before going to sleep and wanted to hear her reassuring answer. That continued for years. Nobody ever talked about death openly; the whole theme was taboo. I had to work through it on my own.

I became accustomed to often being sick myself. The mold, the absence of good nutrition, the cold weather, the extremely poor quality of winter clothing, and the weakness of the medicines all contributed to the poor condition of our health. One of us would get strep throat first and then two others would follow a few times every winter. Papa never got sick and was a very kind caregiver at evening time. But during the day, it was a real hell, with high fevers and unbearable pain for the three of us. A woman doctor would come to our home for a brief visit, give us a prescription and written permission not to go to work or to school for couple of days, and then she would run to the next patient. I would worry mostly about my mother's health, but could do nothing to help her through the whole ordeal.

One day, a real crisis occurred when I became very ill and the doctor called the ambulance for me this time, not for Mama. They rushed me to the hospital. I remember the words *scarlet fever* and the horror on my mother's face. As usual, my father was much calmer and tried to reassure us that everything will be all right. But I was frightened to be taken away from my parents to a room with a lot of other children, all very sick.

I was sure that I would never see my family again and would probably die there, because of my hallucinations and difficulty breathing, and the feeling that life was leaving me. I felt so bad for my Mama to lose me so soon after my Babushka's death. I also felt bad, because the nurse cut off all of my beautiful long hair and made me look like a boy. But I survived, and after a week or so I was back home, weak and skinny, trying to accept my new boyish look without tears.

CHAPTER TWENTY-EIGHT

My father was away from home a lot. He was a geologist, as I mentioned before, and was involved in many expeditions to far-away parts of Russia. He enjoyed his job and always would bring us all kinds of minerals and stones to teach us about nature. He loved to travel and see all new places, but after Babushka's death, it was impossible for Mama to be on her own with two children. I think he never really found himself again after leaving this job and going back to work at the railroad company. Some real excitement was forever lost for him, but Lala and I loved to have him home every evening and it was much easier for my Mama. She had a very important job as a controller in the local government office all through her life but was very tense many times during her career, afraid of the possibility of some kind of prosecution for any trumped-up reason. Accusations could be made at any time by anyone.

My father liked to tell us imaginary and exciting stories that he would create spontaneously on the spot. One of those stories captured his own scientific mind, and we spent a few years listening to the fiction tale of the "Green Girl" from outer space coming for a visit to our Planet Earth. It was a wondrous story that captured my imagination for many years. I remember always asking my father to please continue telling me the adventures of "Zelionaia Devochka" — the "Green Girl" from the world of other planets and stars, different galaxies, worlds beyond belief. It was the "original story of E.T.," created and told by my father more than a quarter of a century prior to the Spielberg movie. When I saw the movie many episodes seemed surprisingly familiar to me. I think my father had an aptitude for writing, had a very creative mind, and loved children. It gave him a real thrill and joy to watch my sister and me listening to his stories with open eyes and open mouths, as he was opening our minds to a big world around us in the midst of the limited and wretched world that we were living in. What a priceless treat it was for me for many years to come! My sister was too little to remember much of this time, and eventually he stopped telling the stories and spent more time writing something that he wanted to publish. Unfortunately, it never happened and all his writings were lost while we were moving from country to country.

I tried to retell his story to my younger American daughter Natalie when she was a little girl, and she loved it, but I do not have my father's scientific mind and his knowledge or just the talent of story-telling. Nevertheless, I felt connected to my father in this unusual way once and again, and especially with a certain sadness that he did not live long enough to see Natalie being born.

Even with both of my parents working very hard, the financial situation of our family was a disaster by any measure. Their salaries were so small, barely enough for basic needs, that the money only lasted for two weeks. Then my mother had to go around to some friends or neighbors asking to borrow money for the next two weeks. All families had the same problem, and so they would help each other to make ends meet. But it was a humiliating experience for Mama and she was always stressed about the lack of money for simple necessities.

Growing up, we had almost no clothes except the bare minimum. The school uniform was our everyday outfit for my sister and me. Mama, Lala and I only had a couple of simple dresses for summer. Our small armoire for all our clothes was half empty. My sister would wear my clothes and shoes as we were growing up and I don't remember her ever complaining. We had no idea that anybody on the whole planet could experience a different life. Poverty was all around in the almighty U.S.S.R as we were getting closer and closer to reaching the communist goal of communal prosperity.

∞

My first indication of understanding that something was incorrect in my assumption about our condition in comparison with the "horrible world of capitalism" came unexpectedly when I was in middle school.

We all had to read the book by Harriet Beecher Stowe, "*Uncle Tom's Cabin*," and I cried when I read it, as it touched my heart. My teacher in school enforced the notions of the injustice in capitalist countries, and the horrible exploitation of rich people over poor people, especially black people in the U.S.A. It was a twisted interpretation of American slavery as a struggle of the working class of mankind against the wealthy heartless bourgeois and aristocracy.

I had a bad feeling about this country America right away, and felt sorry for the black people who were suffering so much. The confusion came when the teacher would compare our great country, the U.S.S.R, where all people are equal and happy and prosperous, with the living conditions of the poor working people, especially blacks, in America during the present time. I was really perplexed, but obviously not asking any questions. Somehow we, even as children, understood that we should not ever question or doubt (at least out loud), any authorities. I had the unsettling thought that my family lived in the worst poverty, worse than even those poor black people in America! Could my teacher be wrong in her comparison? Does she really know what she is talking about? This episode got stuck in my mind and opened my curiosity to the wider world around me, but only internally.

∞

A couple of years later, I felt that my parents were very unsettled, and perceived that there was danger in the air. I saw signs of fear in my mother's eyes. She began talking in Yiddish with my father, which always was a sign that something bad was happening in our small world.

"What is happening, Papa? Why are you so worried, Mama? Can you please talk with me?"

But they would not explain anything, and only told me,

"Everything will be okay, Ellochka. Those problems are not for children to know." That did not help me whatsoever, and I would try to figure it out myself. I overheard something about Jewish doctors, then about somebody having tried to kill somebody else, and then the name Stalin came up.

One day, my mother's older brother Lippa suddenly appeared in our apartment. He was a military man and lived somewhere far away. I barely knew him at this point. I only had heard that many years ago he was the first one in the family to marry a Russian woman. Back then, Lippa wrote to his Mama, my Babushka, who lived in Rogachev that he wanted to come for a visit and introduce his wife to the family. The whole Jewish community was full of gossip.

"Did you hear the news? Meita's son is coming for a visit with his new wife and she is a *goika*, a *schiksa* (non Jewish woman). *Oy, gevalt! Oy, vey!* Who would believe, such a great *ingele* (boy), *mein Gott*, what a shame!"

My Babushka stood up to all of them and told them to stop blubbering and to prepare to accept this woman with *kavod* – respect and warmth.

"She is my son's wife, it's too late for debates, and she is now part of our family."

Babushka opened her heart to Aunt Valya and made her feel at home. By now, it was already history. They had three sons and a good marriage.

Their older son Boris had just entered the college in Leningrad and came to see his father at our apartment. I did not hear the entire conversation between father and son, but the words "Jewish doctors" and "Stalin" came up. Boris said something to his father, probably against Jews, and suddenly I witnessed something that I had never seen in my life. Uncle Lippa got up from the chair and said very loudly,

"How dare you say this to me! I fought in the horrible war for my country and I continue to serve my country, with pride and all my strength," and then he gave a strong slap across his son's face, and Boris almost fell on the bed. Uncle Lippa ran out of the apartment steaming and slammed the door, and then Boris ran out and I was by myself: astonished, bewildered, and shaking.

What had just happened and why? What do my uncle and some Jewish doctors have in common? What did Boris say to upset his father so much? They hadn't seen each other

for a while and Uncle Lippa is a rare guest here. Why would they talk about Stalin? It took me some time to figure out this puzzle. When I talked to my parents about it, Papa and Mama chose their words very carefully to explain to me that there is a suspicion by Stalin that some Jewish doctors attempted to kill some high Soviet officials. My parents did not believe that it was true and thought that everything would be resolved soon and for me not to discuss this subject with anybody at all. They repeated the last words many times, to be sure I understood. I do not know what I really understood, but I knew it was not good for Jews, for me or my uncle, since he had slapped his son that hard, or for my parents, since they were so afraid to talk about it in Russian, and suddenly spoke the forgotten Yiddish language.

It was only after a few years that I got the whole picture of "The Doctor's Plot" against so-called Jewish nationalists. It was an anti-Semitic provocation fabricated by Stalin. His goal was to accuse Jews of many crimes, to encourage Russians to hate them even more and then to save Jews from the mob and pogroms by deporting them all to a newly created so-called autonomous Jewish community in the most distant part of Stalin's empire, the harsh eastern area of Siberia close to China, called Birobidzhan. Stalin had just executed 13 of the most talented and renowned Jewish poets and artists, and was ready for the last act. My parents understood it as the end of their life as they knew it and the beginning of a scheme that could bring about some kind of "final solution" for the Russian Jews. There was a very subdued and under-expressed panic among many Jewish families, including mine. I felt very uneasy in anticipation of forces that could turn my small world upside down, and my parents would not be able to make their own decisions and save my little sister and me. Even my Papa, so big and strong, a soldier who knew how to fight in a war... *Who is doing this to us, and why?* My parents learned how to reassure me by hugs and kisses instead of complicated explanations and would just say that everything would be fine no matter what. And many times I had to pretend that I believed it to be so, just to make it easier on my Mama. The worry on her face was unmistakable.

∞

But God had a different plan…

Suddenly, in 1953, the whole country of the U.S.S.R. was confronted with the death of their Father and Leader, Comrade Iosif Vissarionovich Stalin. The whole country was in a trance, in shock and mourning. I was lost even more. *People were crying about somebody whom they never even met, whom they do not personally know or had a relationship with*.? Funeral music was playing loudly over the radio speakers everywhere. There were real tears on the faces of people on the streets, including the teachers in school.

They gathered all the students in the multipurpose room, and I felt so small among all those big children, and so lost. The director of the school was talking to everybody and I didn't understand, why everybody around me was so quiet and sad, and I did not know how to feel myself. I was not sad at all. This was not my Babushka who died; why should I cry?

But the music of deepest sorrow was so heartbreaking that it was affecting me emotionally. How can music express my own feelings better than I can by myself? How can this composer express *my* emotions so well? Why does the music tell me my own story about Babushka's death and all that was happening inside my soul? Is that why everybody is so sad and many are crying? I did not cry, but I remembered the music, and my fascination with classical music began. For most of the people of the U.S.S.R, it was the beginning of a long journey of life without a "Father," a road of discovering that sometimes, the death of one person can be a great thing, if that person is pure *EVIL*.

CHAPTER TWENTY-NINE

S talin was dead, thank God, but the evil "cult of his personality" went on.

Having received my education in the government-run system, which was dominated by Marxist-Leninist ideology, I had been trained as a future active builder of the communist society. We had to be submissive and disciplined, with no questions asked and no individual choices made. Everyone wore a school uniform. The young ones joined the Young Pioneers party group and wore red ties. Our slogan was "Are you ready to fight for the doctrine of Lenin and Stalin?" And we saluted to the flag, "Always ready." We learned the poems and songs, like "I am a little girl, I am playing and singing. I never met Stalin, but I love him very much," or "Thank you, Comrade Stalin, for our happy childhood." Stalin and his ideas were the center theme of literature, movies, plays, and music. All the creative artists had to support the Party and its ideology. All the writers had to belong to the Union of Soviet writers and follow a policy of "Socialist Realism" to support the ideas of communism. All the other styles in art were denounced.

All schools had the same curriculum, with emphasis on the history of the Communist Party of the U.S.S.R, math, science and Russian language. The party leaders in Moscow determined the curriculum for the whole country, including which books we could read, which music we could listen to, which movies were allowed to be produced. Everything was under strict ideological control. Portraits and busts of Stalin were everywhere. Religion was outlawed. It was considered to be the *opiate of the masses* and had to be eliminated. The Clergy was persecuted, and many churches were destroyed.

Children were given idols to follow, like the known hero Pavlic Morozov, who denounced his own father for his ties with the contra-revolutionaries.

History was written and re-written many times during my grade school and college years, but we had to study it every year with all the dates and details of all the boring actions of the pre-revolution, revolution and post-revolution times. I hated it with all my might, but always tried to appear to be a perfect student from the outside.

The Communist Party pushed very hard to eliminate illiteracy and succeeded. Great propaganda always came from the newspapers and the limited selection of books. Mostly it was indoctrination and misinformation, except that math and science were taught on a very high level, and were very serious and hard subjects for most students. Teachers were usually very robotic, hardworking, mostly women, scared to death to say or to do anything against the rules and regulations.

Among all my teachers in high school, I only remember three. One was a Jewish woman, who taught an English class using a special Soviet system that made it impossible for students to learn and understand a foreign language. The focus was mostly on endless grammar. Another was a Jewish man, a math teacher, who was bored to death by the many students who couldn't understand his explanations right away. I always felt bad for him, wasting his life in the classroom. He was obviously out of place and couldn't hide it very well. He probably had a brilliant mind, but I presumed that his life didn't amount to anything near what he was capable of. Who knows, what really was his fate, and the fate of his family? I just perceived a real tragic figure in him, trying hard to cope with his situation by being cynical, sarcastic, and very distant from everybody around him in school.

But mostly, I remember and am forever grateful to my literature teacher, who most likely came from a very educated family before the revolution and probably suffered a lot with all the painful changes in her personal life. But for me, she was like a light that diminished the darkness around me, like a window into the different world of real understanding of the Russian classics —Tolstoy, Chekhov, Dostoevsky, and the poetry of Pushkin and

Lermontov. I was ready to suffer through all the other subjects just to listen and learn from her.

Alexandra Alekseevna opened my mind and eyes to the world of books, ideas, hidden emotions and conflicts, the depth of the written word, the possibilities of the human imagination and talents, and the process of understanding human nature. She was my "Russian Yeshiva," my hope that I could educate myself through the reading of literature of as many different writers as we were allowed. She was a real blessing to me, because I understood her strong and encouraging messages and was filling myself with the hope of following some intellectual pursuit. There were very few of my fellow students in the class who loved her or her teachings, and the majority of the students were absolutely lost in her class. I understood later that she deserved to be a professor in some great university, not in an old small local school, but she didn't have the proper qualifications and background, was not a Communist Party member, and I am sure had some additional baggage unknown to me. Alexandra Alekseevna was the first highly intellectual and intelligent person I had ever met, and I could not get enough of her. I have always appreciated her influence on my development as a young woman.

The other part of my life was dedicated to music — my "savior and my redeemer." It came to me as such a strong invitation into beauty, hidden emotions, unexpressed feelings, and a connection to the big world beyond me. I became acquainted with composers who grew close to my heart. They expressed to me the sounds of life and death, of love and struggle, of victory and defeat.

Listening to the music was almost an impossible task in those days. We didn't even have a record player at home. But I remember going to the symphony concerts with my father on rare occasions on Sundays at the Leningrad Philharmonic Concert Hall. What a great gift this was from my father to me! I loved every second of it — the atmosphere, the audience, the beautiful hall, the sound of the orchestra tuning their instruments, holding my father's hand in expectation of the magic that was about to begin. The conductor, dressed in a tuxedo (*Wow!*) coming on to the stage, lifting up his little stick and… I am in a different world. The music is taking me on an emotional roller-coaster ride, in all directions of unexpressed emotions. It makes me so sad that I am about to cry, and minutes later it's gone, and the new melody is coming and the orchestra responds and the journey takes a turn, and suddenly I feel joyfulness and even happiness. I could go on and on about those first interactions with the real world of music and me – I have it all stored inside of me. But what is really important is that the dark world that I lived in could not completely kill the light of beauty and art, knowledge and creativity, could not completely suffocate us into oblivion. Even Evil cannot completely shut the gate of Beauty and Goodness.

In addition to my transformational experiences with literature and music, I also benefited from living in one of the most beautiful cities in the world, where the architecture of the best European masters was impossible to hide from us. There was a tremendous contrast between our extremely low standard of living, poverty, and gloomy hopelessness, and the splendor, magnificence and the pompous environment of the museums and buildings around us.

Entering the Hermitage museum of art and culture, with all of the richness and luxury of the Czar's palace, was a surreal experience for me. *Wow, the very special chosen people could actually live like that?* I thought, looking around with my mouth open. *They lived like only Gods could in some Greek mythology books.* As I entered the exhibits of different artists, I would forget all about the beauty of the rooms and immerse myself into the world of paintings. I would surprise myself how deeply I felt observing the scenes of different lives, eras, landscapes, people, colors, nuances, and crafts. I tried to memorize the names of the artists that I loved, to understand what made them choose those particular themes, aspects of nature, or certain people as the subjects of their portraits. I was especially intrigued with portraits, the images of the real people. Who were they? What were they thinking? What made them pose for hours in the front of the artist? What did the artist find captivating in those faces? Many looked perplexed and unhappy, but on the other hand, there were portraits of royalty and women looking proud in their unimaginably beautiful gowns and men, too, in their splendid formal attire.

And then there was nudity. Children would giggle about it, hide their faces, shy away, but I was completely befuddled as to how I should react. We grew up in an asexual society with no information on the subject — *period.* No questions were asked and no answers were given. This subject was taboo. So, I felt much more comfortable with impressionists, and I fell in love with the French artists and their art. I would go to the museum to see those pictures again and again and again. It was music to my eyes.

With regard to nudity, I overheard from the guide in the museum how artists strived to capture the beauty of the female body, the grace, sensuality, innocence, the enchanting proportions... Well, I had a real issue with these statements, and in my mind, art didn't reflect the reality. I knew a lot about womens' bodies, and it wasn't pretty at all. That kind of beauty wasn't music to my eyes whatsoever. I am talking now about a completely different setting.

Almost all the people living in Leningrad had no showers in their apartments, and so once in a while, we had to go to the communal bathhouses. That was the worst agony for me, the most disgusting experience I ever had. To be clean was not on the agenda even though the communist slogan was "in the healthy body there is a healthy communist spirit." Nobody was ever really clean, by the normal standards. My mother would occasionally come home at seven o'clock at night, grab me, my sister, and some clean clothes, and schlep us in the cold winter evening to go for a wash.

The bathhouse was in a very old building about fifteen minutes walking distance from our apartment. We would stand in the line for about an hour on the stairs, where women with crying children were patiently waiting for their turn to enter the hell-hole on the second or third floor. The stairs were narrow and it was hard for women who had finished washing to get through the crowd going down, since everybody was wearing heavy winter coats. Finally we were in, undressing and entering the huge "hot-like-hell" steamy room. It was here where all my being was in a state of shock and horror. I was appalled by this scene. I saw many nude women of all ages, all shapes and forms, red from the heat, overweight and out of shape, short and tall, some skinny like sticks, everybody looking ugly to me, taking a little wash-basin with hot water to the rows of benches, squeezing in and trying to wash themselves with a limited amount of water and a lot of very cheap soap. Then they had to stand in line to change the water, and most of their children were crying and screaming nonstop all that time.

My Mama had a hard time getting through the routine in the hot, humid, and steamy atmosphere, where we could hardly see each other. After the whole working day without time to eat supper, she had to wash us first, when we were little. We had long thick hair and needed a good wash, so it was hard work for my weak mother. She usually would nearly lose consciousness in the process and would be taken outside by some kind woman to breathe some fresh air and would be given an ammoniac to bring her back to life. We had to repeat this horrifying ritual once every few weeks. And I certainly had no admiration for the beauty of female nudity for a long, long time after this.

Sometimes, Mama would ask her co-worker and close friend Anya to come along and help us through the process. They had known each other for many years, suffered through the siege of Leningrad together, and always tried to help and support each other. Anya was an attractive Russian woman with a big loving heart, younger than my Mama but still not married. She suffered through many maladies after the war, never fully recovered and sadly, died very young. I loved Aunt Anya and was so grateful for her kindness and for her helping my mother through this inhumane ordeal, as well as on many other occasions.

It was hard to come to the cold dressing room, where Mama had to help us put all our clothes, including boots and winter coats, and then take us outside to the brutally windy cold night and schlep us back home. No wonder we were sick a lot. The only better part of the whole event would happen at home, where my father finally would be helpful and patiently comb our tangled hair and Mama would have some hot tea and we would be falling asleep in no time, dreaming, probably, about a better and easier future.

∞

The brightest moments of my childhood came when my parents decided to use the privilege that my father had, working for the railroad company: free train tickets for the whole family. They decided to go for vacation to the best place in the whole entire U.S.S.R., a small town called Anapa on the Black Sea. What marvelous trips we had! Those were the best childhood memories for my sister and me.

The sense of the big world, traveling south for about three days and nights through the countryside and looking out the window at the sights was absolutely amazing. There were so many places to discover in the world. We traveled through big and small cities, on the old fashioned choo-choo trains, stopping at different platforms while older Russian women rushed toward the train with some prepared food to sell, hoping to earn a few rubles for their families. Their simple food, such as boiled potatoes with dill and pickles or pierogi, smelled and tasted so delicious — an unforgettable experience.

I remember my first time seeing the Black Sea. The sound of free flowing water was music to my whole being, my soul and mostly to my ears. The sandy beaches, the joy of learning how to swim, the sun, that burned our skin without any protection, the taste of the grapes that we discovered along with so many other fruits, seeing our parent's unconcerned and undisturbed faces, a feeling of pure joy that I experienced for the first time in my life.

Those were the fleeting moments of our lives that stay with us forever, unpretentious memories of our young parents of so many years ago, that we continue to carry with us all through our lives.

CHAPTER THIRTY

When I was eight years old, I heard for the first time in my life, a little girl — the daughter of my parents' friends — playing a piano. I even remember the name of the piece, the composer and the music: *"Clowns"* by Dmitri Kabalevsky. I was a very impressionable little girl and wanted to play the piano like my friend could right away. From this day on, I was begging my parents to buy me a piano and give me piano lessons. My father was a very musical man who loved to sing, loved opera, and also enjoyed listening to music on the radio. He always regretted the lack of opportunity in his life to learn to play a violin or a piano. My mother loved music, but had no musical talents and, surprisingly, could not even carry a tune. They must have thought that after a while, I would forget all about my request. But I kept nagging and begging. The problem was that they had no money to even think about this expensive proposition, given that they barely managed to survive on their minuscule engineer salaries with both working full-time jobs.

They brought in barely enough money for food and other very basic necessities, let alone any luxury extravaganza, such as a piano. But, I reasoned, the other girl had her piano... why couldn't I? Who would be able to explain to an 8-year-old girl that the war had only recently ended, but Stalin was still very cruel and alive, and so many other complicated concepts? I simply had a passion in me and couldn't stop pursuing my dream, endlessly nagging and begging.

I never gave up. One day I overheard my parents quietly talking with each other and the word *"piano"* came up. I immediately stopped moving and tried to listen to their secret discussion. Mama said that the only way they would be able to afford the cheapest piano in town is to spend some money that had been saved to buy her a winter coat. Winters in Russia are brutal, and my Mama had no warm coat, so she was often sick. Papa wouldn't make the decision, saying that it was Mama's decision to make, not his. As sad as it sounds, when I heard this, my hopes were up— the selfishness of a child! After a few days, my parents told me that we would go to look for a piano. This was the happiest day of my life up until that moment, since we never had any toys or luxuries at home. To have a piano would be heaven on earth!

But the piano that we bought at this point was not a piano that the Russian bureaucrats would eventually keep me from taking to Israel. My parents bought a very primitive, simple, and cheap piano. It was definitely an unbelievable luxury for me, and I enjoyed playing it for quite a few years. I remember feeling guilty about my mother, when winter came, but the joy of having piano and taking lessons overruled any other emotion. I became accustomed to this substandard piano, and tried the best I could to advance and prove to my parents that my Mama's sacrifice was worthwhile.

Until the age of fifteen, I never mentioned to my parents the inferior quality of my piano, but at the advanced level that I had reached by that time, I really needed a better instrument. We all agreed that we would search for a new one. We invited our tuner, a good friend, to help us to look for a special piano. It took a long time before we came across a very old piano with a German name that looked like an old, broken-down piece of furniture that was ready to be thrown away. It was a black, old-fashioned upright from the previous century in horrible condition, with broken keys. It had not been tuned for many years, and we were not impressed. *The worst piano I have ever seen in my life*, I thought to myself. But at the same time I had a strange feeling, that there was more to this piano than my parents and I could see. It was just an intuition, a sixth sense. At this moment my tuner turned to me and said,

"I highly recommend you buy this piano."

What? How can he suggest such a thing? What is the matter with him? I have a better piano at home! The only appealing features of the piano were the beautiful candelabras in the antique style of the last century. Unfortunately, even they were worn-down and slightly broken.

"This is a *Schröeder!*" my tuner exclaimed excitedly.

"It was built in St. Petersburg (later Leningrad) in the last century by a fine German piano maker. It has a unique quality, and is a special 'opus' —it even has a few gold medals glued to the back board inside the piano." He showed us the medals and explained to us how lucky I was, what great potential this instrument has, how I would eventually come to thank him for it, and how I would come to treasure it all my life.

The owners told us that the piano had belonged to a pianist before World War II. After he was drafted, the abandoned instrument stood alone in this apartment all through the blockade of Leningrad — forlorn, forgotten, neglected, and unkempt during horrible cold winters in the abandoned apartment with broken windows. Germans had bombed the city every single day. The pianist never came back from the war, and new occupants eventually moved into his apartment. For many years, the piano had been standing there untouched by the new residents, and now they had finally decided get rid of it. They had no idea that behind the broken-down façade was a real treasure (also invisible at this point to me). But our piano tuner insisted that he could repair everything and bring this piano to the glory that it deserved. "You will love the sound — it will be incredible!" he told me, getting more and more excited, contemplating his plan to restore this gift from the last century. Germans were making the greatest pianos of all. I cautiously trusted him and told my parents to take a chance and go for it.

What a great decision it was! Our piano tuner worked very hard to bring this "invalid" back to its previous glory. When he was done I was in seventh heaven! The restored piano had the most beautiful rich tone that only the best instruments possess. The fortissimo was thunderous, while the pianissimo was breathtakingly tender and vocal. I loved this piano with all my musical soul. I entrusted it with all my emotions and frustrations. Many times, I spent hours and hours preparing for my recitals and cried when after endless hours of work, I seemed unable to attain the goal that I had for myself. But sometimes, I had the thrilling feeling of achievement when finally the music would come to life. I had such a personal relation-ship with this piano. I shared my teenage moods, my ups and downs, my discovery of myself, and came to relish my ability to play with real feeling, coming from the depths of my soul, when the instrument became one with me and was very sensitive to my touch and expression.

As the years passed, I began to teach my students on this piano. I fully understood why this instrument had earned a few gold medals, but for the life of me, I could not understand why the Soviet rules prohibited me from taking it with me to Israel. The piano belonged to *me;* it was *my* instrument. After all, it was my friend and I who had brought it back to life out of ruins and had treasured it ever since. It was a painful and emotional parting for me. Finally, I had to leave it with a friend of Sergei and never heard about it again. In truth, I would never come to have a better instrument, and I still miss it very, very much.

My piano studies were humble in the beginning. There was a very good system of music schools in Russia with highly qualified teachers. But my working mother had no idea about all those nuances and was looking more at the convenience of bringing me to the piano lessons. She found a "House of the Pioneers" close to her work place and signed me up, without having any recommendation for a good teacher. I went through a few mediocre teachers who taught me very basic piano literacy, as I tried my best to be a good student and practiced diligently. But they were not inspiring teachers. They were overtired women, who sometimes would fall asleep in the middle of my lesson. I didn't complain to Mama and thought that all teachers must be the same, anyway. My progress was unremarkable, but the teachers were happy, telling my Mama that I was a very talented girl.

After a couple of years I was transferred to Natalia Vvedenskaya. By her name and her demeanor, she probably came from the same bourgeois background as my literature teacher in school. She was a much better pianist than my previous teacher, and I learned a great deal from her. I spent more time practicing and was truly enjoying the results, playing more and more difficult pieces of classical music. But it was not a real music school with great teachers, competitions, or classes in music history, *solfeggio,* and music theory. And so despite all of my dedication, I lost many years of valuable musical training during my childhood while my future friends in college advanced to the highest levels of musicianship and piano playing.

Fortunately, one day, out of the blue, my teacher Natalia decided to tell my mother that I was just wasting my time, that this was the wrong place for me, that I was too talented to be in this poorly organized place, and that I was succeeding despite this mediocre school and it was time to move on. I have no idea why it took her so long to give this encouraging information to my Mama, but I appreciated her finally putting me on the right track. She gave us the telephone number for one of the best teachers in the entire city of Leningrad and told us to go for an audition. Natalia hoped that maybe Seraphima Samsonovna Olchovskaya would take me into her class, despite the intense competition.

I had very complicated feelings about this new development. I was excited, but afraid. I felt unprepared, not ambitious enough, not ready to be challenged, feeling as though I was lacking talent, and afraid of failure and rejection. I was not thinking about a music career for myself, despite my father's recommendation to consider it. He would love for me to become a composer or a pianist or even a teacher. I argued with him, trying to explain that these are his *haloimes* (dreams), not mine.

"Nobody becomes a composer," I tried to convince my father. "You are born to be a composer, and teaching children the musical alphabet one hundred times would be boring, and more than I could ever bear!"

Oh, how I was wrong. I thank my Papa every day of my life for the best suggestion anybody ever gave me. He gave me the best gift that a father could give to his daughter. He helped to find the best profession for me, a career of teaching piano, which I have enjoyed from my very first student, little five-year-old Mashenka, when I myself was only sixteen, to the present day.

But back to Seraphima Samsonovna… I went for an audition and she told me straight to my face that I am a talented girl, but I am doing everything wrong, had bad teachers who did not teach me much, and she will take me only on the condition that I will fully dedicate myself to the hard work of practicing a few hours every day without any complaints or tears. She was quite a lady, this Jewish teacher of mine. She had a real passion for music and the patience of a true teacher. She was a huge influence on my entire life, my character, my choices, my education, my emotional strength, my profession, and my musical soul. Studying piano with her was a very excruciating and trying experience for me with many tears hidden from her, much pain, uncertainness, mistrust of my abilities and hard, hard work. It was training for life. She pushed me over the edge many times, but I learned how to stand and to be strong.

The first six months she never said a positive word about my piano playing. Everything was wrong, poor quality, underprepared, even though I worked many hours every day and tried my very best. I was not good enough. I didn't understand what the composer wanted me to do. I had bad technique, my fingers were not moving fast enough, my legato was not right, and my staccato was not sharp enough. I could not do anything right…and then one day, she looked at me and smiled for the first time. I could not believe my eyes. Really? I did something right this time? It was an unbelievable sense of accomplishment, of a victory, of reaching for the stars…

Seraphima Samsonovna was not just a piano teacher for me. She was my mentor and my guide, and everything that I ever learned, including how to be a good teacher, I learned from her. Most of all, I learned how to relate to music and how to play the piano not just with my fingers, but also with my spirit and my soul. I was not able to attend the music school where she was teaching; at age fifteen I was too old for the system and so she gave me private lessons at her apartment, which was an hour ride on an overcrowded bus ride from our place. And every trip for her lessons was a real treasure, for which I am forever grateful.

CHAPTER THIRTY-ONE

During that time, the Cold War with the U.S.A. was going strong. We were taught to hate our imperialistic enemies, all those blood suckers of the proletariats, those heartless capitalists, smoking big cigars and putting their feet onto the tables. The whole image of the American people was distorted, caricaturized, and negative. Our collective goal was to catch up and overrun this imperialistic America economically and, in twenty years, to build a real worldwide communistic society for the first time on the planet Earth. The words that the government officials used were so inspiring, promising, encouraging, and motivating that a lot of people wanted to believe in their sincerity. I did not know yet what to believe, but it started to sound like *bobe-maices* (nonsense) to me. Except, suddenly in late 1957, the U.S.S.R. launched the first man-made satellite, Sputnik, and we all felt such an unbelievable pride. We were actually winning against the Americans!

Stalin had died five years prior to this moment and Khrushchev had recently come to power and started his crusade against Stalin's "cult of personality." Suddenly, our Teacher Stalin was not so great after all. Stalin had made a lot of mistakes, but he, Khrushchev, would correct all the wrongdoing and Russians finally would win on all the fronts and would become the leaders of the entire world. The next big event was planned as a showcase of the Soviet cultural superiority, this time in the world of art — the first Tchaikovsky international music competition in Moscow. I was fully engaged in my studies and music, when unexpectedly, this event turned my whole world upside down.

Papa had bought our first black and white TV a few years prior, but as amazing as it was, we didn't watch much, since it had only one channel and the programs were not so interesting to us. Papa liked to watch some sports — soccer, or as we called it, football, was his favorite. But everything changed for me when the proud Russians started to transmit some of the parts of the music competition onto TV. The picture was very foggy and unclear, the sound was awful and squeaky, but back then, we didn't know any better.

For me, it was a real miracle. Our tiny apartment suddenly became a concert hall with live young musicians, the best in the world, playing the most treasured classical pieces. I was glued to the TV and then… how can I describe this breathtaking moment? How can I find the words to recreate the miraculous appearance of this young lanky, tall 23-year-old pianist with a big blond curly head of hair? His name was Van Cliburn, but Russians pronounced it Vun Cleebern. He came from America! He was an American! He started to play the piano like I had never seen or heard before. I was enthralled; to me, he was a rock star, before I knew any rock stars — handsome, gregarious and incredibly talented. He gave a magical performance of the *Piano Concerto No. 1* by Peter Ilyich Tchaikovsky. His technique was extraordinary.

But to me, he also projected something new: the warm demeanor, open emotions, artistry and innocence of a free expression, and a hope for endless possibilities. I was just some teenage girl in my room, but he impressed me so much and his musicality moved me so greatly. I discovered a world of perfection, a world of beauty, a world of admiration for such unbelievable talent. I felt that he came from a different world; he was different than anybody I had ever met. For me, he was the discovery of somebody from America who did not fit the picture I had been forced to believe in. Van was mesmerizing and charming at the same time, and it sparked my fascination with America for the first time.

I was inspired, and did not want the event to end. He was clearly the best piano competitor that year, but the question was, would the Russians allow him to walk away with victory? The organizers went all the way to Khrushchev to ask for permission, as we were anxiously waiting for the results. Khrushchev agreed. It was a great victory of talent over dogma, and I felt an unbelievable hope for a more just world. Unfortunately, it didn't stop Khrushchev from the confrontation with Kennedy over the Cuban Missiles a few years later, where we feared that a full blown nuclear war was near. It was a dangerous time, but fortunately, an agreement was reached between the bully Khrushchev and wiser Kennedy.

I have taught piano to many students in all three countries in which I have lived. I have always tried to become at least somewhat more than just a piano teacher to them. It is a very rewarding profession that has given me a lot of satisfaction. It has given me ways to relate to the young generations and to bring the love of music into their hearts. I also had the incredible experience of learning independence and entrepreneurship, creating my own business on my own turf. It was an extremely gratifying endeavor on both fronts. But most fulfilling was to be able to successfully guide all my students, especially a few of them who eventually decided to become musicians or teachers themselves. I have learned a great deal from both my students and their parents in different stages of my career. Times were changing, as were so many aspects of our lives and our priorities. I could write much about my long journey as a teacher and my experiences on this road, but then it would be a whole new and different book...

CHAPTER THIRTY-TWO

A nother enchanting year went by. Our life in Israel was becoming almost ordinary, but extremely enjoyable and outrageously happy. Sergei insisted that in addition to being a mommy for Anat and baby Jacob, I should enroll in a one-year course for Russian musicians and teachers to help us integrate into Israeli schools. I would have preferred just to have some private piano students at home. Although I felt that I'd had enough of schools in my life, I reluctantly agreed with his position. I can see what great advice he gave me. It helped me so much in my future life's endeavors. Did Sergei have some extraordinary intuition or perspicacity? I would never know...

It was time well spent and I learned many new concepts that were missing in my education in the Soviet Music College I attended, such as Dalcroze Eurhythmic, which was a method of teaching concepts of rhythm, structure, and musical expression using movement, and Carl Orff's approach to children's musical development, known as Orff Schulwerk. Fortunately, knowing these two methods would play a decisive role in my future life. My Hebrew also improved dramatically. I was ready to go to work in the fall of 1976, and it made Sergei very happy. He wanted to see me being an active part of Israeli society, and to become the independent and strong woman that he always believed I was when we were in Russia.

Sergei was a brilliant Renaissance man. He always struck me as so different from everybody I knew back then. His intelligence and the influence of the European culture through his parents were apparent and very attractive to me and to our friends. He had an unprecedented curiosity in his soul, a passion for new knowledge and a zest for life. His knowledge of world literature and poetry was deep and thoughtful, and he had an extraordinary ability to recite poetry from memory. More than that, his interest in and knowledge of music was astonishing to me. He knew and loved operas and the classics, and remembered and listened to arias and concertos with all his heart. But even more unusual, he loved American jazz and knew all the great jazz musicians and their music. The old records that he was able to collect in Russia came with us to Israel. Jazz was almost prohibited to listen to in the U.S.S.R. for most of his life, but he would listen to the muffled sound of his old short wave radio through "*Voice of America*" from his teenage years. Beyond that, he knew all the famous French *chansonniers* (singers) and would sing all their songs to me in French — what a cherished treat that was! He was self-educated in world history and philosophy, theater and art.

One of the first presents he bought for his children in Israel was an encyclopedia of History of Art in Hebrew with more than ten beautifully illustrated serious books. I couldn't read those books at all, but he would put Anechka on his lap and read and explain everything that he knew about all those art treasures. It was so many years ago, but Anat still remembers those first lessons with her father. He had a keen sense of the perfect beauty of nature.

Sergei relished his discovery of the incredible history of the Jewish people for the first time in his life. Coming to Israel also afforded us the opening of so many new horizons. We could read all those prohibited books and *Samizdat* (hand copied reproductions of censored publications) of Soviet authors whose works were not published in the U.S.S.R.. We were like sponges for new information, new traditions, new Israeli music and foreign movies. Despite all the hardship of his childhood and youth, Sergei's spirit was very high and pure. It always seemed to me that he treasured every moment of our life, and didn't even want to waste time sleeping. He was hungry for more knowledge, more information, more music, more of good food and wine, more of everything. Above all, Sergei had a passion for politics and the intellectual discussion of old and new ideas in the world, and especially in Israel.

We had achieved an unprecedented harmony in our personal life, where by Leo Tolstoy's definition, "Happy families are all alike." Every day was a real blessing from morning until night. Our children enjoyed a perfect childhood, and we adults created an atmosphere of pure joy in every moment. Our Russian experience started to move into the memory of the past, and we didn't want to dwell on it. Our new life was taking over with the contentment of a day-to-day routine and peace of mind. Well, I am taking back the idea of having peace of mind. We had it in our family life, but the life of the country was a different matter.

We were searching for answers to very difficult questions about Israel, its neighbors, wars, and so called "peaceful agreements" with enemies. We did not trust people to begin with, and it seemed to us very immature to shake hands with those enemies in hopes for a better future. We saw peace as an unachievable dream for the generations to come, not a reality. Sergei didn't want to be pessimistic, but in his view, the Israeli cabinet was extremely liberal and weak, Golda Meir's kitchen meetings were shtetl-like without a clear vision or operational competency. We loved Menachem Begin, Meir Kahane and their ideas, but most Israelis at that time were charmed by liberals.

What was much more disturbing for us was the ideology, political, and economic structure of the country at that time. This was where Sergei was ready to cry. A considerable number of those liberal Jewish communists who were a big part of the Russian Revolution evidently came to Israel and never changed their ideology. They reminded us of Sergei's father and his never-ending dreams of Utopia, where everybody is holding hands and singing Kumbaya, kissing and hugging each other in unconditional love and social justice and equality.

All those socialistic tendencies in this young country made us nauseated. In some *kibbutzim*, portraits of Stalin were taken down resentfully just a few years prior to our arrival! Israel was basically a National Socialistic State with goals, philosophy and ideology similar to the Russians. Leftists in Europe and in Israel believed that communism in Russia were just somewhat misguided, but not fundamentally wrong. It was simply poorly implemented by Stalin, who just happened to be an Asiatic despot and ruthless ruler.

The *Histadrut*, or Federation of Jewish Zionist Workers, a trade union, was established in 1920 and has continued to flourish to the present day. This very powerful organization with its whole system of rules and regulations was stopping innovation and progress. The emphasis on *qiuyt* (tenure) was killing competition and initiation of anything new.

The upper management hated the new young Russian engineers who came to work enthusiastically, having many new ideas to improve the old systems. They looked down on all bright, experienced, and highly educated new immigrants and stood fast against their initiatives. They had tenure, and the power was on their side. The managers were primarily from Poland and Romania and they couldn't stand these newcomers from Russia. Most of them were older, and competition was a threat to them, so they tried to do everything possible to put the new Russian emigrants down. That was an unfortunate situation that Sergei and Mark both experienced and had to endure at their jobs.

The government also had a whole list of privileges and discounts for new immigrants, which only created more antagonism between locals and newcomers. We thought it was another stupid move on the part of the Labor Party. We didn't expect or desire those discounts on buying things such as cars, mortgages, equipment, and so on. It was certainly helpful financially, but did not help to create good relationships between people. Sergei was told to come to Israel with a driver's license from Russia to have the biggest discount for a new car, but he ignored this suggestion. Who was thinking about luxury items at that point in our life? We couldn't buy even a used car for the next few years and we survived. But later emigrants came with ideas of taking full advantage of all privileges in all possible ways. Why not? People are people, and they act accordingly with the legality of the rules set by the governments. But many Israelis were angry with us, misplacing the source of the injustice. We couldn't understand the real purpose of these policies.

The *Histadrut* was the largest employer in the country and owned most of the economy. The bureaucracy eerily reminded us of the one in the U.S.S.R. There were not many signs of the capitalism that we had expected to see, coming out of Russia. But socialism was flourishing in Israel. I saw

Sergei suffering a lot of pain and discontent. After the war economy that had stalled growth, government expenditures rose significantly. We listened to news, like everybody else in the country, and heard new words with new meanings — *inflation, devaluation of the lira, tax increase, tax reform, Knesset.* The many political parties fought endlessly with each other. Sergei saw the Labor Party as arrogant and corrupt, with absolutely uninspiring leadership. They were ignorant socialists, and we were extremely disappointed.

In the midst of all this happiness and pain, Sergei came up with a wonderful idea. "Let's ask your parents to watch the children for a month and we will go to Paris!" *Wow!!* Mama agreed right away and Sergei wrote to Uncle Yanek. *We are coming to Paris!!*

CHAPTER THIRTY-THREE

How to find the right words to describe the exhilarating, magical and triumphant moment in the life of two people in this breathtaking experience of magical proportions? I have lived a long life by now, but I never ever experienced anything like this. Nothing else has been even close! I will thank God forever for giving me this moment. It gave me the strength to go through life with unbelievable gratitude.

Oh, Paris...

I was holding the hand of my Beloved, stepping into the land of his dreams, the city of his parents' youth and memories, places he knew by heart in his imagination, and had longed to visit his entire life. The stunning beauty of the architecture, endless rows of the charming restaurants and cafés, the elegance of the stores, the flowers, the handsome men and the exquisite women, fashionable clothing, the store windows, the museums, the shows, the atmosphere, the air, the food and wine, the older women who were so well-groomed and relaxed, the *joie de vivre!* (joy of life!), the most beautiful language on the whole planet. One of the first things Sergei did when we got married was to teach me how to read French. I could read all the signs and advertisements without understanding any words. The music — the combination of the emotional melodies and French words — was pure indescribable pleasure for our tortured souls. Young careless couples kissing on the corners of the streets, parks with so many people leisurely walking or sitting in groups, smiles...

We are in heaven, in the twilight zone, hugging each other in disbelief. This was never "in our cards." We were not supposed to be here, we were not born to experience this kind of happiness, of joy, of love, of freedom... We were born into slavery with an axe over our heads! We looked at each other and into Paris's eyes. We saw each other for the first time in a different light. We are just a man and a woman in love and in

Paris, and nothing else matters. We can let ourselves just *be* in this moment, intimately, enjoying the time together with no worry about the rest of the world. People can live like this?

Paris was our real honeymoon, after ten years together and two children at home. We experienced the lightheartedness that we never had, the joy of being together, holding hands, laughing like children, with elated spirits, flying high in euphoria, feeling very young, careless, attracted to each other in new and undiscovered ways, having fun, taking pictures for the memories of this best month of our lives.

I understood what harmony and having your soul mate by your side means while in Paris. Great composers could express it in their music so eloquently, deep from inside their souls, with all the nuances and poetic touches, with creation of the melodies that would have a way to bring those emotions to our souls. Words can barely do it, maybe only in poetry.

We treasured every second of the Paris experience with tears in our eyes and smiles, with genuine excitement and melancholy, with sadness mixed with joy, and with wonder and true love for each other and for our life. We felt at home, belonging to this new world in some unexpected way, felt in peace with our surroundings, blending with everybody easily, without trying. Sergei certainly was a Parisian at heart and felt the presence of his parents with him. But even I had the same feeling of melting into the strangely familiar atmosphere. We felt the same blissful energy...

Oh, God, thank you for this unique treasure, for bringing my soul mate into my life and for letting me experience and understand what this life is really all about. We cared for each other so deeply, and with such strong devotion. We couldn't get enough of each other; we were best of friends and best of lovers, we could share our thoughts and emotions, knowing that the other would understand with all his heart and all his soul.

Oh, God, please, preserve this moment! I don't want it to end, my heart is jumping even now — please, don't let it end. I knew, that it would never be the same, never... the music would change... the blissful moment would vanish... the perfection would be destroyed... the whole happiness would flee. Memories would follow me all my life... I would dream about it so many times… I would try to remember the endless love in my heart and my soul… tears… smiles…your tender touch…my Beloved…my pain and my heartache …my harmony…reaching for the joy of US… reaching for you… Oh, God… Please…..

One evening, after wandering about the charming boulevards of the city, we found ourselves in the area of the "Grand Opera," one of the most memorable corners of Paris. After a long captivating moment of admiration and delight of observing the architecture and the crowd, we stepped up the stairs to see the posters and the programs of the events. "*La Traviata*" by Giuseppe Verdi was playing this evening and we jealously watched the stunning, lucky, and happy crowd of Parisians and tourists walking through the doors in anticipation of the wonderful performance. My pulse was beating hard just from the fact, that I was standing among this exclusive public. In Paris!

Unexpectedly, about ten minutes before eight o'clock, a couple of Japanese men turned to Sergei and tried to explain to him something fast in broken French and in some kind of frustrated politeness and in a hurry gave Sergei two tickets, saying "Go, go! It starts in ten minutes!" and seeing us bewildered, not understanding and not moving, trying to figure out what is happening and asking how much money they want for the tickets. Finally, both of them rushed into the theater, waving their hands, showing us to follow them and disappearing into the crowd.

With a strange feeling and trepidation we rushed through the door and nervously showed our tickets, not knowing what to expect. The lady at the door took our tickets and looked at us very suspiciously. I can imagine her absolute surprise seeing one of the best seats in the theater in our hands. To say that we were underdressed for the occasion is an understatement. At this time in history going to the Opera, especially the Paris Opera, was a big event for everyone, with people dressed up to the hilt.

But the biggest surprise was the moment when two ladies separated Sergei and I and one of them took me to the fifth or sixth row in the orchestra and as she was showing me the empty seat, she automatically opened her hand for a tip and I was embarrassed by the whole situation, shaking my head, having no money on me to give her. I passed a couple of luxuriously dressed people and got to my seat one minute before the lights went off.

The next minute, when the overture started and the curtain went up, I abruptly lost myself into the most inspiring experience I have ever had. I forgot immediately the unusual circumstance that brought me there and even that Sergei was not by my side, sitting somewhere else in the theater far away from me. I was in heaven. The dazzling performance, the emotional story with the breath- stopping music that I knew so well, the human emotional and passionate drama, the famous arias, the best voices I ever heard in my life, the amazing sound of the orchestra, and the beautiful costumes! I got fully lost into this occurrence, letting myself just melt into the splendor of the moment, soaring, like in a dream that never ends. For the first time in my life, I was seating so close to the stage that my musical soul almost left me and got onto the stage to partake in the unfolding story. I was all ears, taking it all in, like I never had before.

During the intermission, overwhelmed and emotional, Sergei and I went around to explore the most gorgeous interior of the theater with its excessive decorations, multiple columns, and statues, bronze busts of composers, a most magnificent central chandelier, and impressive stair-wells. *Wow!!* Even Hermitage paled in comparison to this palace, in my mind!

After the performance was over and all the applause stopped, we had a hard time coming back to earth. Great art has the ability to lift us up to heavenly experiences and an opportunity to appreciate the unbelievable God-inspired talent that some artists have. We felt drunk from happi-ness, thankful to those Japanese strangers, laughing at the comical situation that so unexpectedly gave us one of the best evenings of our life. What a memorable evening!

∞

We stayed with Uncle Yanek and Aunt Simone in their nice apart-ment in Louvicenne, very close to Versailles and about 25 minutes away from Paris. They both were wonderful hosts and did everything possible for us to feel welcomed and at home. Everything was so French and new to us and so beautiful and rich. Their older daughter, Jacqueline, and her husband, Maurice were our guides, giving us a beautiful tour of Paris. At nighttime, the views were especially magnificent, and Maurice provided us with historical context and interesting explanations. Their younger daughter, Arlette, invited us for dinner at her house one day. *Wow*, it was the first time in our life we had entered a private European house. It was shockingly beautiful, spacious, modern, light and luxurious, with stylish furniture, an out-of-this-world kitchen, bedrooms and music, and then the dinner was served in the green flowery back yard in the French style and the most delicious food! *Wow!!*

The whole family was together in a relaxed atmosphere of confidence, peacefulness, joy and tradition. Everything seemed so rich and expensive. *Oh, this is how some rich people live in this world?* I thought, without any under-standing that it was really just a middle-income family. We thought that they were very, very rich to live in a separate house and entertain their guests so lavishly. Many years later, Anat, after visiting Paris, told me that Arlette's house was not big at all, smaller than our house in California. I was shocked. Really?? Coming out of Russia, our perspective obviously was distorted about a lot of things…

Arlette and her husband Leon invited us to join them for a day of sightseeing tour to the *Chateaux de la Loire*. I think they enjoyed seeing their Russian relatives discovering the new aspects of life, our innocent admiration of things that were so ordinary to them. For us, everything was new, a discovery of the world. The castles were so majestically full of grandeur, masterpieces of the Renaissance in France. Strolling through the picturesque gardens was a delight. But just driving with people that were so comfortable in their own skin, relaxed, confident, having enough money in their pocket, knowing exactly what they want to show us, where to go — that was a discovery by itself.

And then, our first ever lunch out! The prestigious atmosphere, charming ambiance, the pleasing waiters, the best wine and the mouthwatering classic French cuisine dishes… We are in heaven again, living our dream life. I remembered Tosca's story at this moment, and my heart clenched. I started to understand her much better than before my own experience of her world. I stepped into her shoes, maybe for the first time. How did she survive without losing her mind, coming from Paris and being forced to live in Russia? That day was another brilliant page of our life. I thought that I would never want to lose my ability to be child-like, open-eyed, open-minded, and excited about the world around me.

Sergei suggested leaving Paris for a few days and going to London. That was a great side trip, and we loved every moment of it. Just to be able to move freely from country to country was a thrill, but to visit London? Who would ever believe that we were actually able to go there? We had another few days of unbelievable discoveries, except we didn't know any English and felt very touristy. We were running around from morning till night nonstop, so excited to see with our own eyes all the amazing places that we had only read about or seen in pictures. However, after a few days we were already missing Paris, where Sergei's French was very helpful for us. Back to Paris…

"How many days left?" I asked Sergei. Certainly, we missed our kids and the family. It was the first time we had left them for a whole month. But the truth was that we didn't want to go back to Israel. We would much rather live in Paris, where we didn't feel the anxiety and stress of day-to-day life with all the Middle Eastern complications. Sergei and I felt much more relaxed and calm in Paris, and he was developing a plan to open his heart to the family. We decided to talk to Uncle Yanek and the rest of the family and see if they would be able to help us to move to France.

We were not interested in the politics of France or their government. We were not very curious at that time. We just felt that it would be a good idea to at least talk to Sergei's relatives about the possibility of moving to France. Unexpectedly, Arlette was not receptive of this idea at all, and the rest of the family agreed with her right away. "You are Jews, and all Jews are better off living in Israel. We can't help you, because it is a very complicated process, and we think that it is not a good idea. A second emigration?

Not knowing French? What about your families in Israel? To start a new life again?" Nothing made sense to our French family.

Sergei continued the argument for a little longer, but I didn't understand their discussion in French and could not participate anyway. Later, after Sergei's translation, I was surprised at how this logic about Jews applied to us, but not to them! But now, after so many years have passed, I am glad we didn't follow our unrealistic idea, and I understand Arlette much better.

One thing became clear. We had to say goodbye to Paris, to our wonderful family and reluctantly get ready to go back to Israel...

CHAPTER THIRTY-FOUR

Coming back home was a bittersweet experience, and a part of our hearts was left in Paris forever.

I started to work in the Israeli public schools as a Eurhythmic teacher in the fall of 1976, and I really loved it. The delightful children responded so enthusiastically and freely to the musical experiences, exercises, songs, and improvisations. It was my first time to teach (in Hebrew!) so many children at once — a completely different experience from teaching piano. I also had my share of private students at home. So, I became very busy and active with a lot of help from my Mama and my sister Lala, who was staying home with her little son Avi.

We traveled to see the countryside. We were very impressed by the exciting, energetic, and urban city of Tel-Aviv. But most of all we were overwhelmed by our first trip to the heart of Israel, Jerusalem. What an unforgettable experience that was! There is no other city in the world like Jerusalem. You can feel the presence of infinite energy only there, and the feeling stays with you and around you as something very unique. Being in one of the oldest and most sacred cities in the world makes one aware of time and history, and you start feeling it within your own being. Jews have lived here, on and off, for about 3,000 years. *Wow!* We went to the old city, stepping on the stones of the narrow street of "Via de la Rosa," where I finally witnessed the place where this "Russian guy Iissus Christos" was carrying his cross before the crucifixion.

The next place was the Western Wall or *Kotel,* the Wall of Tears. I was trembling without realizing why. There are just no words to describe how I felt, but the vision of the spirit of my ancestors was in my heart. Sergei went to the men's half of the wall, where many religious Jews were involved into deep prayers. I slowly came to the wall on the women's side and touched it with my hands, feeling the unusual coldness and warmth

of the stone at the same time. To my surprise, I saw many little pieces of
paper all over the wall and figured out later that people write their prayers
and make pleas to God on those papers and hope for God's help. My
prayers to God would come many years later, when I would also come to
the Wall with my own little note and my own heartfelt prayers. But back
then, for my first visit, I just was standing there, feeling only this unique
energy flowing all through my body and experiencing the rare mystical air
of the unknown-to-me presence of God.

We went to *Kibbutz* Schluhot on many occasions and loved to spend
time there with Eliezer and Menucha. Every time, it was the most uplifting
experience full of mutual love, joy, Shabbat celebrations, good food, interesting conversations, especially since our Hebrew was getting better and
better. I felt very close with Eliezer and Menucha. Their warmth, kindness
and religious values deeply touched my heart.

Our apartment in Kyriat-Yam near Haifa was located ten minutes away
from the Mediterranean Sea and so going to the beach was an easy trip
during the weekends. It was great to see our children and their cousins
being so excited about life and growing up together as best of friends.

Our mixed feelings continued unchanged. The wonderful happiness
of our family's life was in direct contrast with the chaotic disarray of Israeli
politics and economics. We didn't see a good future for the country and
worried about our children. We didn't like the direction of Israeli government or some members of the Knesset, and we grew even more and more
critical and tense. There was no change on the horizon for the better. The
feeling of living in a land that was surrounded by a tight circle of enemy
countries was unsettling and we didn't see any good solutions for the future.

The summer of 1977 gave us a little hope. The election of Menachem
Begin was somewhat of a turning point in Israel. The Labor Party was
defeated after 28 years in power. We wanted to see a real change, including

the reduction of government control and the power of *Histadrut*, the powerful labor union, to begin with, as well as elimination of the inequality between Sephardic and Ashkenazi Jews. We were expecting real leadership from the Likud party, and changes in the economic structure too. But at least for the first time, we were a little less pessimistic about our new homeland.

CHAPTER THIRTY-FIVE

The next picture in my mind is a beautiful afternoon near the end of June, like so many others. I had made a very nice lunch for the kids, and they were sitting and waiting at the table, talking and laughing, and we all were in a great mood. I had just served lunch when the telephone rang. "Geveret Okun?" a voice asked, "Your husband is in the Rambam Hospital in Haifa and we would like you to come here as soon as possible." Then — silence.

What? Did she say that Sergei is in the hospital? Did I understand her Hebrew correctly? Why is he in the hospital? He never was sick and felt great this morning. Did something happen? What happened? SERGEI??? Oh, my God! Electricity surged through my body, something was pounding in my head. I didn't move for a few minutes and absolute silence surrounded me. Then I heard the childrens' voices again in the kitchen. Wait a second... the voice had said that I have to come to the hospital immediately. Now my whole body was shaking and I heard my heart pounding in my head – *hurry, hurry, hurry!*

I called Mama and asked her to come as soon as possible to watch the kids.

"Why, what is the rush?"

"I don't know anything and can't explain, but Sergei is in the hospital." She ran as fast as she could and I told the children that I would be home soon.

I remember the sickening feeling inside of me growing by the seconds as I was crossing the street, walking as fast as I could toward the bus station on this very hot afternoon. The sun was overpowering, bright, ready to burn, to scorch. It was hard to breathe, to move and to think. The one hour ride on the bus was endless, and I felt like I was on a rollercoaster. My thoughts were all over, jumping from one to another — imagination, anxiety, fear and voices inside nonstop, talking with each other. *I am sure it is nothing serious, it can't be anything serious, why would it be serious? But why did they ask me to come? They wouldn't ask, if it isn't serious.* I closed my eyes, trying to calm myself down, counting the minutes to the end of this long, long, torturous ride.

I entered the hospital and somebody helped me to find the right place.

"Geveret Okun, please wait, and the doctor will be with you in a minute."

A young good-looking doctor introduced himself and simply told me that my husband had "*Atkafat Lev*" a few hours ago. My medical Hebrew was very limited, mostly on children's sicknesses. I didn't know what "*Atkafat Lev*" was, so it didn't shock me right away. But I saw his concerned eyes and felt a sense of seriousness about the whole situation.

"Can I go to be with my husband?" I asked.

He responded patiently; "I am sorry, but not at this moment. We are trying to do our best to stabilize his condition. Try to relax, Geveret. I will let you know."

He left me standing there in a state of affliction, despair, and disbelief. I felt my heart was starting to break, but at first I couldn't cry. I couldn't even process the information, hoping that I translated everything wrong in my head. I don't remember how, but somebody finally told me that "*Atkafat Lev*" was a heart attack or "*infarct*" in Russian.

I stepped outside. *O, My, God...this is not happening!! No...No...No!!* I knew what a heart attack was, but Sergei never had any problems with his heart before. He was never sick, he was skinny, he didn't smoke, and he lived a healthy life style. *Why, why, why is this happening to him, to me, to our children? Yashenka is only 2 years old!!* Tears were running down my face and I felt so sorry for all of us and mostly for my Beloved...I wish again I had known how to pray, to say a *Mechaberah, Rephua Shleima* — a special prayer for the sick and a speedy recovery. I wish they would let me be with him, to hold his hand, to tell him that our love is stronger than any disease, that this is just a temporary nightmare, that everything will be all right.

Later that evening, the doctor told me that I should go home to rest and come back the next morning.

"We are doing the best we can to help your husband," he assured me again, "But we need more time before we will let you see him. We are cautiously optimistic." I wanted to scream and tell him, that it is my Beloved he is talking about. He is young, we just had our first trip to Paris, we love each other, doesn't he understand? It is his absolute duty to save Sergei; he must do more than everything possible. He must do the *impossible* if necessary!!

I was screaming silently all the way home and all the way back to the hospital the next morning. I obviously couldn't sleep that night, crying quietly, trying not to wake up the kids. I experienced an empty bed for the first time in my adult life.

The doctor looked perplexed, with the same concerned eyes. There were no real changes in Sergei's condition yet. After a couple of days, he was slowly beginning to show signs of some improvement and there was a sense of more hope. Walking outside the hospital I found a treasure — the hidden window of Sergei's room, which I could carefully peek into. I saw Sergei in the hospital bed eating breakfast. What an amazing gift to see him again! He looked good, handsome, young and stronger than I expected. After seeing him I was sure that he would win this battle. And he did.

Coming home from the hospital was a real celebration. Happiness all around, the kids were so glad to see Abba (Daddy) home again. We knew that recovery would take time and we were ready to take things slowly, gradually. That was a humbling experience of adjustments. It was hard for Sergei to take life easier, to rest more, to work less, to stop throwing Yasha into the air, to go to sleep earlier. After a few months, things started to become more normal again.

We visited the best cardiologist in Haifa, who happened to be an Arab doctor. After the checkup he assured us that everything looks very good, despite this troubling heart attack. He gave Sergei some recommendations and told us to go cautiously back to normal life as soon as possible. Two recommendations I remember: to eat fewer eggs and to walk at least 30 minutes every day. Unfortunately, doctors didn't know much about heart disease back then.

From this day on, we never looked back and lived as if nothing had happened. Sergei felt good, didn't take any medications, walked, ate fewer eggs and more veggies and fruits, and went back to work full time. We returned to our pre-cardio infarction life, full speed ahead.

Looking back, it is very strange to me that we never talked to each other about the whole episode. We tried to avoid the discussion about our scary feelings of uncertainty, never considered the possibility of another heart attack, and never, ever touched the subject of death. I wish we had talked more about these things. I wish that Sergei had shared with me some of his thoughts, his perspective, and his desires for the future of his children, and for me. I wish I could have heard from him his own fears or anxieties, his understanding of death. I wish I had been able to explain to him my terror of losing him, of waking up in the middle of the night, listening in the darkness to be sure that he is breathing.

But because of our twisted Soviet past and absence of knowing God, religious pursuit was not in our life at all. We wanted to be strong for each other, and talking about death was a sign of weakness. We were protective of each other in the strangest way, ignoring heart-to-heart confessions of our real emotions. We were very warm, caring and tender with one another, but couldn't have an in-depth conversation about life and death. Unfortunately, we had grown up with the mindset of, "What was there to talk about? You live, you die. Tragic, but that's how it is."

Many times in my thoughts, I have tried to go back to those couple of years of our lives. Sure, I was worried about Sergei's health, watching him carefully, trying to do more so that he would do less, trying to protect him from stress, from political discussions, from getting overtired. But never openly, verbally, never asking questions, just looking into his eyes for answers, avoiding any upsetting conversations.

There was only one time in our entire life together that we got into a real fight.

One of the first things Sergei decided to do after the recovery was to learn how to drive and to buy a used car. He wanted to travel more, to see more, to have more fun, to learn a few new things. He did all of this in a very short time and felt so happy about it. I was apprehensive — too much stress, Israelis are horrible drivers, he never had driven before, he was not experienced, we had lived without the car for a few years — he should take it easy. But Sergei had already purchased the car, and it was parked outside of our building when we had this discussion, so I had no choice but to accept this new reality. We started going a few places close by, and I tried to worry less.

A few weeks later Sergei told us that we were going to visit his mother. Tosca lived about an hour north of us. I absolutely panicked. He had never driven so far away, and it was Friday afternoon with a lot of traffic on the roads. I was afraid of the unbelievable stress that Sergei would put on himself and told him that I did not want to go, and I did not want him to drive so far away. He looked at me in amazement, expecting that I would be thrilled to do it, not understanding whatsoever, what my problem was. I didn't want to tell him the truth about me worrying so much about his condition and thinking that the stress would be too much for him. He wasn't about to change his mind at all and was so excited, telling us to get ready. I didn't know what to do, what to say. It was a very unusual situation, where I absolutely disagreed with my husband. Fear was taking over.

When Sergei once again told me to hurry, suddenly tears started flowing down my face. All the emotions, hidden inside for so long were pouring out of me as I was sobbing and talking, trying to convince him and sobbing more and more. I was a mess. Sergei, bewildered, as most men would be, came to console me without really understanding why I was so upset and hugged me, reassuring me that everything would be just fine.

And it was a great trip. Tosca was thrilled to see us, we had a nice Shabbat dinner together, and everybody was happy by the end, especially Sergei.

That was the one of the very few episodes that little Yashenka remembered about his father. So ironic, that of all possible episodes of our life this episode of the unusual and rare tears of his mother got stuck in his head for life...

CHAPTER THIRTY-SIX

I n our entire life, we had never met anybody from America and we knew nothing about American life, economics, or politics, except for all the anti-American propaganda we had heard in the U.S.S.R. We also thought that for some unexplained reason, it was a very rich country, but a very violent one with a lot of scary crime. Still, we had a lot of curiosity, and even admiration about America. We heard from some friends who had relatives in America, that it was a country with golden opportunities, abundance of freedom and unbelievable beauty. New York seemed like a pure fantasy, not a real city, more like a city on another planet.

We had the impression that Americans were the most unusual creatures that had the privilege of being born free and living their lives in a completely different dimension that we had no idea about. We would like to know English, but at this point it seemed completely unrealistic to learn it.

Unusual circumstances brought some new experiences into our lives. Just before Mark and Lala left Russia for Israel, my mother asked them if they would be so kind as to meet an older lady, a friend of hers, for a short conversation. The old Jewish woman begged them to take a couple of very old family treasures to some long-forgotten relatives in Jerusalem.

"It is my mission to send this *Kiddush* cup and a few other items that were kept in the family from generation to generation. I don't have children," she said, "So, I must send it to my nephew."

When they were still in the *ulpan*, Mark telephoned the elderly woman's nephew Bibi, and he and his wife Tamar came from Jerusalem to visit them. It was a very touching meeting and Bibi, a professor of geology at Jerusalem University, was very happy to receive the gift and love from his elderly aunt whom he had never known. Just before they left the *ulpan*, my mother asked Tamar where she was born and where her parents were

from. Tamar told my Mama that her parents were from Belorussia, from
the *schtetl* of Rogachev.

"Really? What an unbelievable coincidence. I am also from Rogachev.
What is your mother's name?"

Tamar said the name, but it didn't ring a bell with my mother and
everyone, surprised by the whole event, said *shalom* to each other and they
left, promising to stay in touch.

All during the night, my mother couldn't sleep and was thinking about
her childhood in Rogachev, a Jewish *shtetl* where she spent all her earlier
years and teens. Images of her family, aunts, uncles, and her parents were
filling up her head. Most of the family members were killed during the
war, but who were those people she could barely remember that left for
America?

She tried again and again to figure it out and by the morning she came
to my sister and said,

"We are from the same family. I remember now." She drew a family
tree and explained the connection.

"Tamar's mother was from the other side of the family, but I remember,
when I was a very little girl my cousin Sadie, who was much older than me,
with her young husband Abraham and their two young daughters, Ida and
Lily, decided to leave for America. Sadie was the daughter of my uncle
Berl Farberov, my father's older brother. It was a big shock to everybody.
She was a very young, beautiful woman and her parents tried to stop her,
crying, begging, and trying to scare her into staying.

"I barely recall the day when Sadie came to say a tearful goodbye to
the whole family. What I remember most of all," my mother told us, "is
that Sadie lifted me up, hugged and kissed me. She also said, 'Remember
me, little Pesia, I am leaving to go to America, but I want you to remember
me, would you?' She looked happy, but was crying and it was confusing
to me. I liked her a lot and didn't understand why she is going to America
and what is America, anyway? I didn't know if I would ever see her again,
because everybody around me was also crying, especially my uncle, her
father, and her mother."

Mark called Tamar in the morning and told her the story and explained to her that we are all skeptical about the connection, thinking that after so many years, Mama could put too much of her imagination into the whole story. Tamar, surprised as she was, said that she would definitely talk to her mother and would get back to us.

The next day Tamar called and told us that Mama's story apparently was true and that Sadie lives in New York and has four adult children and one grandchild. Tamar was the daughter of a sibling of Uncle Berl's wife, and so she was related through marriage to Sadie. It was such an unbelievably happy day for my mother, to find a lost relative, in America, after so many years. She immediately wrote a long letter in Yiddish to Sadie and was nervously anticipating her response.

To her surprise, she received a quick response from Sadie's two younger children, her son Harold and his sister Annie. They wrote that their mother was in the hospital in grave condition. But they read the letter to her and she was absolutely elated, happy and unbelievably pleased and relieved. All her life, she had wanted to connect with her family, to see her relatives who immigrated to the U.S.A, and especially to hear about her parents, whom she never saw again after she had left them so many years ago.

Harold was in the U.S. Army during World War II and happened to participate in freeing some of the concentration camps. At the request of his mother, he would scream at the top of his lungs, "Is anybody here from Rogachev?" But nobody ever answered. And now, near the end of Sadie's life, she had the happiest surprise. Little Pesia is in Israel with the whole *mishpucha* (family)!!

Mama wrote a few very long and detailed letters to Sadie, telling her many stories about the family, filling in the gaps for Sadie, some history, many anecdotes about different relatives, and Sadie's parents' hardship of losing their connection to their dear daughter, whom they never saw again. With a lot of sorrow, she wrote to Sadie about the war and the tragic death of everybody who stayed in Rogachev, including all the members of her family. More questions were coming and Mama was writing more and more until one day the letters stopped. Sadie had passed away.

She was in so much more peace after making the connection with my mother, her cousin from Rogachev. Before she died, she asked Harold and Annie to promise her that they would meet us in Israel, accept us into the family, and help us as much as possible.

Harold, a Princeton graduate, was a professor of psychology at New York University and requested his sabbatical year in Jerusalem to be able, in line with everything else, to fulfill his promise to his mother and to meet us.

I remember the day he called me on the phone and told me that he was in Jerusalem and would come to Haifa next Thursday to meet the whole family. We were so excited and immediately started preparations for our "State Dinner, Russian style," including a lot of different appetizers and then a full three course dinner with some vodka and famous Baba's cookies, my Mama's recipe, for dessert. We didn't know what Americans eat, what they looked like or what to expect altogether. But "professor from American university" sounded very imposing and even intimidating, and so we all were full of excited energy and anticipation.

On Tuesday late afternoon our doorbell rang, and I went to open the door, asking in Hebrew, "Who is it?" I heard a man's voice, saying, "This is Harold," and my heart dropped. Harold? I opened the door in complete panic and saw an older man wearing a baseball cap, not looking American at all to me, standing there, ready to introduce himself and give me a hug. Still in a state of shock I let him in, hugged him and said "Harold, today is Tuesday, not Thursday!"

I couldn't communicate with him, not knowing English, but I understood right away that I had mixed up those two days, because they sounded the same to me. It wasn't funny – the reception that we were planning didn't happen and we didn't greet this American relative of ours in a full-blown Russian tradition. But it became kind of a funny anecdote in our family, laughing at me, "Is today Tuesday or Thursday, Ellochka?"

Harold was nothing like what we expected, and didn't fit into our imaginary picture. He was a brilliant intellectual Jewish man, but he didn't look American. I guess I expected a distinguished looking gentleman with grayish hair; a tall, movie-like image of a rich man with a cigar, a beautiful suit, ready to put his expensively shod feet on the coffee table. I remember my first thought, as I opened the door, was, *This is probably Harold's chauffeur, and Harold must be sitting in the car, waiting for us to come and greet him.*

How wrong and naive I was about the world, and about the country that eventually would become my home. I was idealizing this country from the time of Van Cliburn, and his image became my prototypical image of the American young man. How distorted and delusional my head must have been at that time.

In any case, we had a lovely dinner together, during which my mother and father mostly spoke Yiddish to Harold, and we were asking a lot of questions through my parents. Mark's English was pretty good, so he was actively pitching in. In the middle of the conversation, my little Yashenka turned to me and said, "Ima, please say something! You are so quiet, I am afraid that Harold would think that you are dumb." I think that is when Sergei decided, that we should start learning English. But it wouldn't happen for the next few years.

This visit became the first in a sequence of many visits during Harold's stay in Israel. We became very close and big admirers of his, even without a common language. We became good friends and part of his family. Harold had a very comfortable demeanor, a great sense of humor and a world of knowledge that I could only imagine. I wanted to talk with him so badly, to ask him my entire collection of questions, to debate his political stands, to know more about the freedom of speech that we heard Americans had, and so many other subjects.

My fascination with America grew by the minute now, after meeting Harold. I always felt that America was the best and the greatest country in the world, but I couldn't figure out exactly why. I thought that Americans were a completely different breed of people. Harold and then Annie, who came to visit us a year later, were the most delightful, joyful, kind, and down-to-earth normal people, but they had a very different experience of life than we did. I could sense it right away during their visit to Israel,

but even more so, when I came to America, and they became a huge and
instrumental part of our new life.

CHAPTER THIRTY-SEVEN

I have met so many extraordinary people in my life, and they have each touched me in a deep and most unique way. Some of them have become dear friends for life, and this is the extraordinary blessing that I treasure most of all. One such person, Boris Poliakov, became the closest friend I ever had.

Sergei and I were just newlyweds when my best girlfriend Irina from Music College called me and told me that she would like to come for a visit and to introduce us to her new boyfriend. She sounded excited and urgent at the same time. I invited them to come for dinner on the weekend.

I remember seeing Boris for the first time as I opened the door. *Holy cow*, I thought right away. He was the most handsome man I had ever met. He had dark hair and blue eyes, with a disarming smile and unusual charm. Irina introduced us, and Sergei invited them in. Our friendship started right away — the ease, the conversation, the discussions, the understanding, and the warmth. We were on the same wave length — close hearts and close souls, like we had known each other for a long time. I was so impressed by his incredible intelligence and knowledge, and by his taste in books and in music. Sergei was engaged and happy to find a great mind — another Renaissance man. What a blessing!

In the U.S.S.R. people could impress each other only with their minds and their character. What else was there? Money? Investments? Positions? Real estate? Cars? World travels?

Toward the end of the dinner, I asked Irina to help me with the dishes and we left for the kitchen.

"Irina, dear, I am so happy that you met this wonderful man. I really like him a lot, and I can tell that Sergei is real fond of him, too," I started excitedly. She looked at me and I saw such mixed feelings on her face.

"Ella, I am in love with this man; he is just pure gold for me." She stopped for a minute. "But…" Her tears were precluding her from talking.

"What, what is going on, Irka? Is he married?" I was whispering anxiously, "I don't understand." Finally, she took a deep breath and quietly told me,

"He is sick, very sick."

"Cancer?" I asked, sinking low, suddenly feeling mortified.

"Oh, no, nothing like that. But I think it is even worse. He has muscular dystrophy," she said. "It is a progressive disease. Over time, his muscles will slowly die or atrophy and doctors can't stop it. When he gets up and walks, look at him. He has a strange walk from side to side, like a duck. This is the beginning."

I had so many more questions, but Sergei came to the kitchen asking, if we needed any help. We came back, trying to hide the alarm behind our smiles, and when it was time to say goodbye, I looked at Boris and saw his duck-like walk for the first time. They left, promising to see us again very soon. A beautiful young couple in love…

I was dumfounded, stunned, and confused. I was still at the age when we feel ourselves invincible, and immortal. Sergei wanted to know what was going on with me. Didn't I like Boris, and how could somebody not like him? I told Sergei what Irina had told me, and then we both lost ourselves into sadness and grief. We didn't have Google back then to get more information, so we were just guessing and imagining, what is happening in Boris's and Irina's hearts and how Boris can live like this, and be so charming, and go to University, and continue living… We had just met him, but had already become dear friends.

We didn't need to spend time to become friends, to know each other better. It happened instantaneously and forever. Our feelings were absolutely mutual, and we tried to spend as much time with Boris as possible. He had a room in a small communal apartment in the center of the city, and his apartment became a gathering place for many young people to come together and communicate, talk, discuss, argue, laugh, and cry together. Boris was like a strong magnet for his friends. We met many very interesting and special people in Boris's circle.

It was the late 1960's, and times were changing in the U.S.S.R. Young people were ready for the first time to start to talk more openly, to understand and analyze everything, including the horrific history of the country, rumors and lies, confusion over the evil forces that were dominating the world, political downfall, economical struggles and so, so many other different subjects. Coming out of a long, long silence and fear, young people tried to find others to be able to open up, to speak freely with, debate, listen, learn, and share. We were still very careful and had to be selective as to whom to talk with, but we trusted Boris and most of his friends, though not all of them. We felt safest only with him.

Boris was a great debater, and Sergei, probably for the first time in his life, found a real strong partner. They would have sharp arguments and disagreements while debating the complicated subjects of human existence, perception of history and the reality, human consciousness, the struggle of Good and Evil, the place of the individual, the rights of the people, the place and power of the government.

We were on a quest of seeking the *truth*, going back to ancient philosophers and studying modern writers, especially those that wrote for the underground *Samizdat*. After a whole lifetime of fear of opening our mouths, it was so refreshing and uplifting to be able to express ourselves in an open forum, at least among this small group of devoted friends.

We all listened illegally to "*Voice of America*," despite its scratchy and distorted sound, and started to learn more information and gain more insight about the world. We had heard somewhere that in the U.S.A., people have "freedom of speech and press." *Wow!* What a noble idea this was!! Really? You cannot be arrested or even killed for your own opinion, if it is not in line with the opinion of your government? The upside down world that we grew up and suffered in all our young lives slowly was changing, one step at a time. We would talk about new books and movies, and small changes in the life of the country. We shared our hopes for the future and the problems of our day-to-day lives.

By the end of the first year of our friendship, we knew much more about Boris's condition, and even though he didn't like to dwell on it, it was clear that a dark cloud was hanging over his head and his future life. My friend Irina, under pressure from her family, decided that she couldn't continue their relationship. A future of being with this slowly dying invalid was more than she could bear.

It was very difficult for Boris to realize and accept how bleak his future promised to be. His diagnosis was "muscular dystrophy," and the progression of the disease became more and more apparent. He knew that it meant a slow death of his muscles, which eventually would confine him to a wheelchair, but also to absolute dependency on others, and then to death.

He didn't know how rapidly or slowly the progression would occur, and subsequently, how many years would be left for him on this planet. With all the great friends that he had who were willing to help him with everything possible, by the end of each evening, when everybody went home, he had to face his deafening solitude and silence alone.

Boris had previously been married to a beautiful and talented artist. They had a little son together. The discovery of his condition happened when his mother-in-law, with whom he never saw eye-to-eye, insisted that he go for orthopedic surgery to improve his duck-like walk. The surgery was not only unnecessary, but also detrimental for his disease, which had been sleeping quietly inside of him for all those years.

After the surgery, he was in a cast and was not able to move for a long time. When finally his doctors told him he was ready to walk, something horrible and unexpected happened. He was unable to walk at all. The doctors were perplexed, and couldn't figure out what went wrong. In their opinion, nothing could have predicted this kind of unforeseen outcome that had no explanation. But after many tests, examinations and analyses the new team of doctors came to a stunning conclusion and gave Boris his new diagnosis without much of an explanation, as was very common among Russian doctors.

He called his wife on the phone and asked her to read the description from his medical encyclopedia. That's how, for the first time, he and his wife got the shocking news about his future. Their marriage was not able to withstand the tragic news and crumbled under the stress of this horrific discovery. Unfortunately, they got divorced soon after. They were both shocked and horrorstruck about the future of their son, since it was a genetically inherited disease, with a fifty-fifty chance of their son getting it too in the unforeseeable future.

What an unbearable challenge my friend Boris was facing in his life, what a hardship of inhuman proportions!! What a painful and unfair task he had to face, being alone in a country that had no interest in easing conditions for invalids or handicapped people, veterans of the war, sick children, or anybody else. Nothing was done to ease their suffering in the U.S.S.R. Even to buy a primitive wheelchair was a big problem. There were no special accommodations or handicapped entrances, no conveniences, no cars — absolutely nothing. There was no way to survive, to struggle for a future that was so gray and dark. He was only 27 years old when we met him, but his life was heading to a dead end.

Boris never impressed us as being a pessimistic man. Quite the opposite, he was always upbeat, stimulated, and enjoyed being with friends immensely. But in his own world and in his deep thoughts, he didn't see how he could survive alone.

At one point, when he was walking to the bus station on a snowy and icy street at evening time, he lost his balance and fell down into the snow and hurt himself badly. The terror was that when he tried to get up he couldn't. His muscles were already too weak. It was cold and windy, and nobody was around as he was helplessly laying down there in despair for a long time, trying and trying again and again to get up. And at this moment, for the first time, the thought of suicide crept into his head as the only rational solution for his desperate situation.

I felt torn apart by the whole ordeal, understanding my friend's decision and not blaming Irina for the breakup of their relationship. But being pragmatists, we were lost in trying to find any solutions for Boris's situation. It was a heartbreaking time for all of us and I cried to the heavens for answers with no reply for a long time.

∞

But God had a solution. Unexpectedly, He brought a real *angel* into Boris's life.

Vera had come into Boris's life unnoticed, quietly, with love at first sight on her part, but with no recognition on his part. That was long before his first marriage, when they were very young. They were friendly with each other, but he didn't recognize her as anything special at this time, and their lives drifted apart. She never stopped loving him, but didn't have any hope for them ever being together. She got unhappily married for a few years to a man whom she didn't really love, just to distance herself from Boris. But she kept her first love alive in her heart for all those years.

They met again in the crucial time of his life, where he was dangling between life and death. Vera knew right away that her destiny was to be with Boris, for better or for worse, no matter what the future would hold. She had no hesitation, no doubts, and no second thoughts. Her real true love for Boris was as strong as ever, and this time, she was ready to fight for it with all of her determination. And they fought about it for a long time. He couldn't accept this gift from heaven. He understood that her life would be a full submission to his needs and wants, the life of a slave, attached to him and helping him day and night. She would have to be attached to him through the unbearable pain and progression of his disease, following him slowly to his death. She would never be able to have children, freedom, or her individual desires.

Boris would rather die than let Vera stay with him. He tried to explain to her again and again, that he could not accept her kindness, her sacrifice, or even her love under such terrible circumstances. He couldn't understand at this point that for Vera just to be with him, to love him, to live with him, to help him as much as she could was all that she wanted in life. For her, it was a blessing. Boris was a blessing. And she defeated him, always with smiles and sincerity, cordiality and spiritual honesty.

I remember how torn we were, watching this incredible struggle of two remarkable people whom we loved so much. Many times in life there are no right answers, just a leap of faith.

Vera was a real angel. Boris discovered it slowly during the progression of their unique relationship. She brought her strong Russian character into his life along with her ability to stand by his side without any regrets, complaints, or tears, even when life would take a sharp turn for the worse. What a bright star, what a pure soul this girl was in the midst of the dark, black sky!

She changed his life, and also the lives of all of us who were his friends. Boris's room became so much lighter, happier, full of good energy, and full of optimism. Vera would entertain everybody with Russian tea, cookies and wine. She was an engineer and was teaching in the technical college, but she had enough time to always take care of Boris first. She found a way to get him a primitive wheelchair, and that was their treasure. He couldn't walk at that time and so she would lift him up from his chair and put him into the wheelchair and take him for walks in our beautiful city of Leningrad.

Vera was a petite and very slim girl, but she was strong enough to lift Boris up for all his physical necessities, in and out of the bed and so much more. She would wake up a few times in the middle of the night to help Boris change his position and relieve him from pain. Her job around him was endless...

CHAPTER THIRTY-EIGHT

Vera knew a few of the stories of Boris's family and their past, but some of his other stories she would hear with us for the first time. He was a great storyteller and we always listened in amazement and sadness. I understood that one of the reasons that Sergei and Boris became so close was a similarity in their background that was so different from most Jews in Russia.

Our grandparents and parents came from the *shtetls*, similar to the life depicted in the movie *Fiddler on the Roof*, which was based on the story written by Sholem Aleichem. Life in the shtetl was a small world of provincial Jews who endured a lifetime of hardship, poverty, and pogroms. Most men attended yeshivas with Jewish studies and held insignificant jobs, trying to support their families. Women were busy raising a lot of children and doing their endless housework. There was no broad education, culture, or exposure to knowledge of the world, music, or literature.

But Sergei's and Boris's parents had lived in Europe, and were influenced by European culture and way of thinking, and what a colossal difference there was!

Boris's story is one of the most unique and tragic that I have ever heard. He was born in 1940. His mother was previously married to an opera singer and had a son. The marriage fell apart after a few years and for the next couple of years, she dedicated herself to working and providing for her child. She was a beautiful and delicate woman, and in 1932 she met Shmerl, who had grown up in Harbine, China, where his parents had run away from the pogroms in Russia in 1906.

After Shmerl's *Bar-Mitzvah*, he left home and for eight months was tramping through Russia in an attempt to find his sister, who lived in Moscow. When he finally found her, he was unrecognizable, sick, and dirty. His sister helped him to get on his feet and study Russian. The year was 1918.

Shmerl went to school to get an education. He was quiet and sweet, but a strong and intelligent man. He met Boris's mother, and they fell in love and got married, planning to live happily ever after. They had a very good marriage with no children of their own, until Boris was born just one year before World War II began. That was the climax of their life together. Shmerl decided to enter the military school soon after they got married, and graduated just in time for the beginning of the war. In June of 1941, Boris's father kissed his son and wife goodbye and left to fight the Germans, never to return home again. He perished without a trace after only one month in July, 1941.

The family — mother, two sons and her parents, were evacuated from Leningrad to the Ural Mountains soon after Shmerl's death. When Boris's older brother turned 18 years old, he decided to volunteer into the army and left, also never to come back from the war. Almost at the same time, Boris's mother was diagnosed with breast cancer and was operated on in the local hospital.

After the end of the blockade of Leningrad, they returned to their city and fought to get their apartment back, since it had been taken over by someone else. Soon after, Boris's mother became sick again, and the doctor explained to her that the surgery had not been done properly. The doctor tried to save her young life, but failed. She died in 1945, devastated that her little Borenka —who she loved so deeply, as only mothers can — after all these tragedies, would become an orphan in this cruel world. And so Boris lost nearly all his family, except his older grandparents, by the age of five.

His grandpa David was a broken-hearted and depressed man. He clearly understood the political situation in postwar U.S.S.R. He was fearful that he would be arrested and refused to leave the house to go to work. So he stayed in hiding, thinking that if he was home all the time, the officials would forget about his existence and would leave his poor soul alone. And so there was only Boris's Babushka Sorah-Rohel who raised him, devoting all her love, energy and soul to him. She was 65 years old by this time and by Russian standards, a pretty old woman. It was a long road of life that she had traveled that brought her to this point.

She had been born in 1880 into a rich Jewish family. Her father was involved in the business of building railroads, and was known as a very charitable man among poor Jews. Sorah-Rohel had an excellent education, including music and Hebrew, could speak perfect German, read a lot of world literature and loved poetry. She was also part of the Jewish social-democratic organization "Bund," and had a very active social life.

She and David were married in 1901 and the newlyweds decided to go to Europe to further their education, using part of her inheritance money. They spent ten years in Vienna, Darmstadt and Berlin, received an excellent education and became parents to three children — two boys and a girl, who would become Boris's mother.

They continued to be part of the Russian social circles and participated in the deep philosophical discussions about the future of Russia and the world. In the "Russian café," she was introduced to Lenin and later to Trotsky and thought that Trotsky was a much better orator. They met and became friends with a lot of famous Russian intellectuals during their ten years in Europe, especially in Berlin. Her husband worked for an electrical company, and Sorah-Rohel loved to spend time with her children and entertain all their friends at their home.

Life was wonderful.

In 1910 David was offered a high position in Calcutta, India, but Sorah-Rohel had heard that there were lots of snakes in India, and she didn't want to expose the children to this danger. Instead, they decided to go back home to Russia, where they had left their families. Babushka Sorah-Rohel also didn't like the fact that the children spoke perfect German, but didn't know good Russian. She had a great deal of nostalgia about Russian culture, too.

When his Babushka was telling him those episodes of her life, Boris couldn't understand what was wrong with his grandparents. To return to Russia? What for? It was hard for his Babushka to explain to him, that it is always easier to see history with hindsight vision. But very few could see and predict the future horrors. Everybody just lived their daily life from today until tomorrow.

They came back to Russia during the time of tribulations before the revolution. Many things had changed during their perfect years abroad. It was hard to understand and adjust to the new, obscure world. But after 37 years of a beautiful existence, Sorah-Rohel had to abruptly turn the direction of her life, like she was born just yesterday. It was the beginning of a new life.

She had to go to work, and all of her prestigious education turned out to be suddenly meaningless. She learned how to sew and became the breadwinner for the whole family, leading the very mediocre life of the Soviet working class. Grandpa David passed away in 1951 and from this point, her full concentration was on raising her only grandson, whom she loved more than life itself.

She gave Boris her undivided attention, trying to be both a mother and a father for him, a friend and a mentor. He was a very intelligent and curious boy. I am sure she was overbearing for him, as he was growing up, and they had a lot of conflicts through his adolescence. But he loved her more than anybody else in his life. She was the only family he ever had. She gave him the unprecedented gift of her broad European culture and knowledge with a clear view of the world. She knew all the best poetry by heart, and he would listen and try to understand and repeat it himself. She gave him the kind of education that he and all the rest of the children of our generation couldn't get in our Soviet schools.

Boris had plenty of disagreements with his Babushka and her philosophy. He was in many ways a brainwashed child, like all of us, and endlessly tried to prove how wrong she was in her perception of the new Soviet system, Stalin, and all the rest. She wasn't hiding her strong opinions from him, like most of our parents did. She was much more fearless, and went to Moscow to meet one of the scariest agents of the KGB, Felix Dzerzhinski, and even Lenin's wife, Nadejda Krupskaya, with some complaints about the unfairness of certain laws and regulations. She was ready to fight for justice. The woman had more guts than anybody I ever met!

It took Boris a while, like for most of us, to start to understand and to sort out the propaganda from the reality. He was a rebellious kid all through his teens, fighting against his Babushka smothering him, striving for more independence and less of her influence. They had a very complicated relationship, but by the way he was talking to us about her, telling us a few episodes of their life together, I knew that deep down in his soul, he loved her completely. Boris admired her, and was amazed by her strength, willpower, and by her outstanding intelligence and wisdom. His two uncles, whom he wasn't fond of, accused him many times of insensitivity toward his Babushka, not appreciating her enough, sometimes being selfish and disconnected, not trying to help her to worry less, and exhorting him to stay home more. But he was growing up, like all of us, trying to find his own place under the sun.

Unfortunately, I never met Sorah-Rohel. She died a couple of years before we met Boris. But I always felt that I truly understood the dynamics in their relationship and the incredible strength of her personality. Her life was that of an unsung hero, just by being able to survive under those tragic circumstances and raise such a wonderful human being.

For Boris, her death was a moment of truth. He felt absolutely alone in this world. Babushka, who gave him all that she could, was not there for him anymore. It was an unbearable realization.

"I am alone, alone!! There is nobody here for me. I have lost my Babushka forever... How will I survive without her? Where will I go, what will I do, when she is not around? Forgive me, Babushka, for all the unintended suffering that I caused you. Please, forgive me. I didn't mean to hurt you. I only always loved you. I am crying now not because you are there, but because I am here...." Life for Boris was never the same without Babushka, but new pages began to open up for him.

A few years after we became friends, Sergei and I came to Boris with the shocking news about our friend leaving for Israel. Boris and Vera were the only people to whom we disclosed this, and we were talking, or rather whispering, about our confusion of what to do and what decisions to make, how to adjust, and how we could leave. They both would want to leave Russia too, but how in the world could they practically to do it?

Vera wasn't a Jewish girl, and we had no information about the acceptance of non-Jewish spouses in Israel. Her Russian family would be stunned by her desire to leave them and Mother-Russia behind. Intermarriages were very common in Russia, and in most cases Jewish men would marry Russian women. Would Vera be able to cut her own Russian roots and adjust to live among only Jewish people with all their specificity, holidays, and different religious traditions? Would Soviets let non-Jewish spouses go?

Debates, pro and con, were going until midnight on many occasions, and enthusiasm was turning to almost depression from one day to another. Vera had no confusion.

"*We* must go after you. When you figure out the situation there, just send us an invitation. Period." Boris wasn't sure, considering that his poor health condition was getting worse by the day. Miracle of miracles happened, and despite all the hardship that Vera had to endure, fighting the Soviet system, the government officials finally allowed them to leave the Soviet Union in 1976.

CHAPTER THIRTY-NINE

A few years later, Boris showed us a couple of chapters of the book that he had been working on. It was an autobiographical story about his life, with a background of the political, economic, and philosophical life of the U.S.S.R. We had no idea that besides all his other great attributes, Boris was a very talented writer in the tradition of the best writers of world literature. We knew that he had graduated from the prestigious Leningrad University and had a Master's degree in history and philosophy. We knew that he was writing poetry, but that was quite a different skill. Boris was anxiously awaiting our review, since we were the first ones to have the privilege of reading the beginning of his book that eventually would have 625 pages.

I loved his writing. It was his very personal story, but very expressive, emotional, deep, descriptive, written with a sensitive play of words and language, as a skilled musician would play a musical instrument. At the same time, I felt that it was also the story of all of us, of all our broken generation, our broken lives.

"Boris, it has such an unbelievable potential! It could become a great achievement for you and for Russian literature!" That's what we *should* have said to him. Instead, we told him, "It's a well-written story, but who in the world would be interested in reading it? Nobody!" We were really afraid that he would use his talent, his energy, his time and Vera's help in vain, because in Israel, with all the problems facing the country, no publisher would ever be interested in our stories, our struggles, and our broken lives.

Being so engaged in trying to build our new life in this young country, which was so new to us, Sergei and I didn't want to look back and analyze our past. We wanted to forget it as soon as possible, almost to erase it from our memory, not ever to dwell on the horrors and oppressions, on the abuse and the pain. We tried to run away from it and start living a different life with none of the past creeping into the present. Reading Boris's brilliantly written chapters meant going in the opposite direction, backward. Why would he even want to do it and for whom would this book be of any interest?

Boris was obviously upset with our reaction, and didn't expect to hear this degree of negativity. Though, we tried our best to be as sensitive as possible in expressing our concerns about publishing this kind of book and affirmed his talent as a writer, Boris disagreed with us. Even if we were right, he carried this book within him and it was destined to be born, no matter what. Thank God, Boris continued his labor of love with the instrumental help of his wife at his side.

Boris gave me many great lessons in life that I took to my heart. I feel his presence at my side and his encouragement while I am on this unexpected journey of writing my own memoir.

Looking back, I understand both sides of this dilemma, but at the time, I couldn't fathom his aspiration to tell such a tragic story that under the pen of a real writer could become timeless, and even essential for the coming generations to read. I couldn't see that the history of humanity repeats itself again and again, because people don't see history as the present and the recent as history. It is all *one*, and today I am afraid that our history can easily be repeated again in so many ways. We lived it and we understand, but the younger generations continue to live in clueless naivety.

Boris's book was finally published in 1985. I received it shortly thereafter, as a gift from Boris and Vera. They sent it to me in America with love and best wishes for my new life. I treasure this book and go back to reading it again and again. Every time, I find in it more depth, nuances, and details that fascinate me to no end. I wish it would be translated into English, but then again – who is going to be interested here and now, except for a few of my friends? It is such a truthful story of our lives, of Boris's struggle for survival, his optimism about life, his ability to find light in the darkest moments of life, his portrayal of his Babushka, his devoted wife Vera and the collective portrait of all of us.

The book was published with the financial support of donations from all their friends, and even contributions from our American charitable friends who never knew Boris, but understood the situation from our stories about him. By the time he finished the book, Boris was fading fast. Almost all of his muscles were paralyzed. He couldn't move, or even breathe. He was hooked to a breathing machine 24 hours a day. He couldn't even talk, and so Vera was writing as he was whispering the words that she had to guess many times just by watching him barely move his lips. What an unbelievable resilience and strength they both had!! Boris's mission in life was fulfilled, and he was triumphant. He passed away in January 1986, and was posthumously awarded the Israel Rafael prize and award for literature. Boris has not been with us for nearly 30 years now, but among his Russian readers, his book is as alive today as it was back then.

The last scene of Boris's book portrays his own death from a heart attack in Russia just before they were about to get a positive decision and permission to leave Russia for Israel. Vera then came to Israel alone and settled in Kiryat-Yam near Haifa. But that is not what happened in reality.

After sending them an affidavit to help them to immigrate to Israel, Sergei and I were under a lot of stress and anxiety, waiting for the decision of the Soviets. We also knew that their absorption into Israeli life would depend on us being able to work with the Israeli bureaucracy. What a glorious day it was for them and for us when we received the positive news. Our excitement had no end. We knew that their life conditions would become so much better than they could ever dream about in Russia.

We met them at the airport after three years of separation. Smiles, hugs, kisses, happiness... We saw changes in Boris. He had gained a lot of weight, was much less mobile, and had grown a beautiful dark beard. But his blue eyes were radiant and his smile was as charming as ever. Vera was full of excitement and curiosity.

It was a real problem to get Boris to our third floor apartment, since we didn't have an elevator in the building. Sergei, Mark and my father put him on a chair — he didn't have a wheelchair — tied him tightly, and slowly and carefully lifted him up step by step, being afraid that they would drop him, and it would be a horrible disaster. It took them a long time and a great deal of effort to manipulate his chair on those narrow stairs. When they finally reached the apartment, we celebrated their arrival with a lot of wine and food, catching up on the endless stories of the last three years.

They stayed with us for about a month, during which time Vera and I were running all around Haifa from one bureaucrat to another trying to get them assigned to a convenient *ulpan* and an apartment on the bottom floor in Kiryat-Yam. After many unnecessary bureaucratic struggles, they moved to a beautiful place, perfectly accommodating their needs and only ten minutes away from us. From this point, all our lives were as ideal as possible under the circumstances. We all visited Boris very often, and my mother was very helpful to him during the times when Vera was at work.

When we returned from our vacation from Paris, we told detailed stories about our trip, trying to help them travel vicariously with us, if only in their imagination. Yashenka was just one year old, and they were happy to have him around. Sometimes, Lala would bring her baby son Avi for a visit, and both boys would delight and bring more happiness to their life.

Boris was obviously missing his son and many of the friends that he had left in Russia, but slowly, people started to come to their place in a similar fashion as it was before. It never was the same, though, as in his youth. Soon after settling down, he started to work on his book.

Boris and Sergei were as close as ever. They had so many new aspects of life to discuss now. Israeli reality was giving them plenty of material for that. We had our Passover dinners together, where Yashenka was singing *Ma Nishtana* (How is this night different from all other nights?), and we were amazed that we were able to participate in the Jewish holidays together openly, contemplating our Exodus from our own Egypt.

After Sergei's heart attack, he insisted that all of us start learning English. Did he have any premonition about the future?? Was he subconsciously preparing me for my future endeavors? Was it an intuition on his part? I can only guess. One of Boris's friends gave him a new system for learning English with some primitive pictures, and we were trying to figure out the system for this extremely complicated language with barely any progress, but with a lot of humor, laughter, and camaraderie.

My parents lived just a few minutes away from Boris and Vera. They visited them, were helping them often, and were a great resource for them. Boris and Vera were like family to all of us.

CHAPTER FORTY

The life of my parents changed dramatically in Israel. They felt at home much more than we did. Yiddish was their *mamaloshen* (mother tongue). They suddenly remembered all the holidays' songs and dances. They enjoyed the Yiddish theater and shows, Yiddish humor, and had no problems communicating with the local people. In some ways, their childhood past came back to life and gave them a second wind.

Going to the stores was very exciting for my parents. There were so many varieties of food they had never seen. But going to the Shook (farmers market) was even better. "Look at the beautiful fish, fruits, and vegetables!" they would exclaim to each other and to me in disbelief. And watermelons? The sweetest we ever tried!

They spent a lot of time helping my sister and I raise their grandchildren. It gave them such an unbelievable joy and happiness. I never saw them more upbeat then those few years out of Russia. There were never any signs of nostalgia over the life they left behind and the country that they spent most of their lives in. Except for painful separation and torn connections with their extended family, brothers and sisters who never left Russia, everything was good.

And we all felt happy, if only for a while...

Sergei and I also took an untraveled and unconventional road for us, people with no spiritual awareness, by signing up for one of the first classes of TM — transcendental meditation — in Israel. With this decision, we stepped into untried waters of exploration that surprised even ourselves. I never knew this adventurous side of Sergei before. He was too involved in life to sit quietly for twenty minutes doing nothing. But we really got into it with a lot of curiosity and even enthusiasm and were following the program precisely every day morning and night.

After a while our teacher of TM told us about an advanced course, where meditation can work real miracles, such as elevating us above the ground. It was an expensive proposition, but Sergei was insisting that we participate, despite the fact that it sounded really weird and "out there." We signed up, paid the money and were ready for miracles to begin with the program starting on the first of September, 1979.

In the meantime, my sister Lala and Mark left Israel to go to Europe to meet Mark's brother and his family. They were in the process of immigration to America and were waiting for their entrance visas in the transitional camp in Italy. During the few years since we had left, emigration from Russia had become completely different. We paved the way, and the masses followed. It was now a much easier process, with easier rules, known information, and much less oppression. Most of the emigrants wanted to go to America, not to Israel, and they were welcomed by Jewish organizations with open hands and hearts and with a lot of help. After meeting his brother in Italy, Mark and Lala traveled to Paris and London and were having a wonderful vacation.

In Israel, meantime, things were not so great. Papa didn't feel good for a while, but didn't complain until I had a feeling that he was hiding pain and discomfort. It was bizarre for me to suddenly become almost a parent to my father, take him by his hand, and insist that we visit the doctor. The lady doctor told me immediately to take him to the hospital, where after all the tests, he was scheduled for surgery for colon cancer. Regardless of who you are or where you are, this diagnosis always stops you cold, and leaves you unprepared, vulnerable and scared.

Sergei and I sat in the hospital during the surgery, waiting for the doctors to talk with us and give us more information. I was worried and sad, and time wasn't moving fast enough. Papa had been so healthy all his life, never was sick and now straight under the knife? I was worried about my mother's health all my life, but she was getting better with age, and was overcoming all her problems. But Papa? I wished my sister could have been with me, but she had no idea what was happening, and we didn't want to interrupt their once-in-a-lifetime vacation.

After his surgery, Papa came back home for recovery, but he was never the same and felt "under the weather" for the remaining couple of years of his life.

On the thirteenth of August we celebrated Boris's thirty-ninth birthday with songs and dances, great food, and toasts for life. All the children were playing outside with their dog Atos. Everybody was in a great mood. There was music, noise, speeches, Vera's happy face, hugs, kisses, Lala's stories about the trip to Europe, presents, laughter, hot weather right outside of their sweet apartment. Sergei had just started his vacation from work and was feeling great, discussing his traveling plans to see more of Israel, to go to the beach and to the new huge pool in the community center.

On the fifteenth of August, Sergei and I went to Tel-Aviv for the beautiful Jewish wedding of Bibi and Tamar's older son — the first real Jewish wedding we had ever attended. We had an interesting and even emotional time witnessing the ceremony under the *Chuppah*, with the rabbi chanting, the groom breaking the glass and everybody singing *"Mazel Tov* and *Siman Tov,"* clapping enthusiastically and dancing vigorously with real happiness in the air. Our own wedding had been a dry official Soviet ceremony, very subdued and unexciting. We were not allowed to have any religious references, not Christian and certainly nothing Jewish. What a contrast!

During the reception, replete with a lot of Israeli food and wine, we were introduced to all the family and friends of the wedding couple. The Russian Kiddush Cup that their aunt had sent as a gift from Leningrad with my family was proudly used for this special occasion. We joined the crowd dancing the *Horah*, and watched the men lift up the groom and the bride in their chairs. Joy was all around and it reminded us of our first *Simhat-Torah* in Leningrad about ten years before. How changed our life was. How unbelievably blessed and happy we felt, smiling and hugging each other, dancing, jumping, clapping, sharing the best of times with everybody around us.

Oh, how wonderful life can be, almost to the point of pain, an unforgettable lightness of being...

On the nineteenth of August, Sergei, the children and I were in Haifa, strolling and window-shopping, buying a few things, enjoying the end of our delightful vacation, just the four of us together. By the evening time, Anat begged us to go to the movie theater and we decided to see a new American movie, "*West Side Story*," which we all enjoyed very much. Tired, but very happy, we came home late and kissed the children good night before going to bed.

CHAPTER FORTY-ONE

I want to stop for a moment and breathe deeply, wipe my tears and relive the harmony of this evening again and again and again. This normal, but beautiful day would never be experienced again by my family. Never again would we have the serenity of this ordinary, but miraculous energy, where love is the essence, where closeness is cherished, where eyes meet and souls rise, and where peace resides...

I had only one last night with my Beloved, but I didn't know. After this night he would never be with me again, *never*...

I would be left alone in the emptiness and coldness, in the awful finality of Sergei's departure from this life, at the point of no return, with nobody to reach out to, to confide in, to hold, to love, to cherish, to share, to hug, to care, to embrace, to talk with. There would be no loving blue eyes looking at me with admiration, no tenderness and understanding without the words, no music of the souls that could only be heard by us.

The pain of this loss would fill me up, consume me and never leave me. The colors of life would simply disappear. The air I breathed would feel as though it was choking me, and the loneliness would be tragic.

I would try to cover it all up by slowly moving through life, saying to myself, "*I can do it,*" and "*I can continue without my Beloved.*" I held the striking grief inside of me so that nobody would know. I would reserve the pain just for myself, because nobody would ever understand what it meant to me... I didn't know... I didn't know... I wish I had known...

I would hurry up and tell Sergei the whole story of my life without him. Maybe then he wouldn't leave me. Maybe then, he would fight even stronger to stay alive. Maybe then, he would bargain with God for more time. Maybe he would beg God to stay with me and our children for a little longer, maybe... *Why in the world did it all fall apart?? Why did he leave us so soon?? Why did he become like a ghost of the past??*

Sergei, my dear, my Beloved, my Love… As long as I live, you are alive in my heart. You have never left me, or maybe I have never left you…

∞

The morning of August 20th was sunny and bright, and we had made our plans for the day. After breakfast, Sergei decided to spend a little time repairing our washing machine that had some problems. He was showing little Yashenka how to do repairs, teaching his son the first lessons of manhood. I walked by, enjoying the scene and making some happy comments about the two men, big and small, working together. This is the second and the last episode that our son would remember about his father. He was only 4 years old.

Suddenly, suddenly, suddenly — I heard the strong sound of wrenches falling to the floor. I was close by and ran back to the laundry room. Sergei became very pale, and with a weak voice, ,said that he didn't feel good and had to lie down. With my heart beating like a drum in my head, I helped him to the bed and called the ambulance. I looked at Sergei and felt the grave moment of this inconsolable abyss.

"Please, please, do not succumb, do not give up. I love you so much!" I said those words, looking at Sergei and feeling his pain. I saw it in his face without him saying a word.

I spent the whole day in the hospital, talking with the doctors and nurses, begging them to help him as much as they could and more, but the truth is that they had very few solutions in 1979.

One time, they let me into the room, saying that he was feeling better. Sergei looked at me with a smile for a minute, told me that I looked very nice in my new blouse, and wanted to say something else, but abruptly, an alarm signal from the monitor went off, the nurses ran into the room to his bed, and I was hurriedly ushered out of the room into the corridor, where I was trembling and shaking from this experience. Despite my shock and raw emotions, I wanted to go back to be with Sergei, to hold his hands, to ease his pain, to add my healing energy to his struggle, to look into his eyes, to protect him, to reassure him, to tell him how much I love and need him. But the doctors wouldn't give me the permission to enter Sergei's room again.

Time was standing still, and my heart continued pounding very hard in my head...

Tosca, who was feeling sick from the news about her son, and was barely moving, came to the hospital and then Sergei's brother Victor, and then it was evening...

Mark came to be with me later during the evening, and I was talking to him just to talk, not to think, not to do anything, just waiting for this nightmare to be over.

At about 11:30 at night I heard a lot of noise and nurses running and through the open door I heard the doctor screaming "Sergei, Sergei, *Ata Shomea Oti*, can you hear me?" He repeated it a few times very intensely and loud. I thought that they were trying to give Sergei an electric shock or something like this. A nurse saw me and Mark standing in the corridor and witnessing all the commotion and asked us to immediately go further outside, and she closed the door behind us.

We were standing in the cold, dark, and quiet corridor outside the cardiac wing for some time and then the door opened and the nurse called us to come in. As I slowly started to move toward the doctor, who was standing and waiting for us in silence, I lost my consciousness and fell down, with the last thought,

Sergei is gone, he is no more...

Oh, my God!!

The music stopped... The unfinished song of my sorrow....

Chapter Forty-Two

There was fog and blurriness for the next couple of days, unfocused vision, some shadows around me, screaming stillness. I saw my mother and my sister coming and going, doing something, talking on the phone with somebody. Our friend Lena, a doctor, was giving me some capsules to swallow, somebody was asking me some questions about some arrangements for the funeral... Funeral?? Oh yes, now it is time for the funeral, but I still was in shock, and around me was just fog. Suddenly my memories of Babushka's death were back, and my feelings were so painful, so deep, so unreal.

I remember that I didn't see my children. They went to our friend's home overnight. I made the horrible mistake of not taking them to their father's funeral, trying in my poor way to protect them from the trauma. It was very difficult for Anechka... My heart was broken, but hers was also. Unwittingly, I repeated the mistakes of my mother. I was still the product of my past.

Funerals in Israel have to take place quickly. A Jew must be buried within 24 hours after death. I remember my father sitting on a chair at home, very thin and pale, with tears in his eyes. He couldn't go with us to the funeral because he was very weak after the surgery and just hugged me, trying to give me some words of encouragement. I still remember his sad eyes looking at me in disbelief. My friend Lena gave me a shot of some tranquilizer, I remember vaguely, and somehow, I got to the cemetery.

There were a lot of people around, but I didn't recognize anybody. My body was there and moving, but it felt like my soul was far, far away, maybe even with Sergei... The fog continued. I remember sitting down on the bench by a woman, a neighbor, and she gave me a hug. She was crying loudly, and saying some words like, "what a tragedy, your husband was so young, so nice, so special." I heard her sobbing in the fog and I was surprised that she was crying so hard. I couldn't cry. I was just frozen, numb.

In Israel, deceased Jews are covered in a white shroud without the coffin. Remember, I had touched Babushka's dead body, and the coldness created in me a fear of death that lasted for years. Well, this time I touched Sergei's covered body, and it was warm from the sun. But it felt wooden, not like Sergei's body at all.

Sergei was gone, and somehow, experiencing his death, my fear of death dissipated and was also gone. I didn't fear death at this moment. I feared life…. life without my Beloved…

The ceremony over the grave seemed long. The rabbi or possibly somebody else who looked like a rabbi cut through the collar of my black shirt, and then he and the others joined in prayers and chanting. I was shaking and stood with closed eyes most of the time, afraid that I might collapse again.

When the funeral was over and I left Sergei behind, it hit me again — the finality of it, the end. The last cord of our unfinished life together had been cut.

The following morning, Anechka and Yashenka came back home, as I was lying motionlessly on the sofa. I saw Anechka's grieving face, and hugged and kissed them both. Then the tears came for the first time, washing my face as I was coming back to live a different life without my Beloved, but with our beautiful children, who needed me now more than ever. That was the first step of acceptance for me. I had no alternatives, and didn't have the luxury of falling apart. Sergei's life was over, but mine had to go on. I still had a life to live, and children to raise.

I meditated alone, without Sergei by my side. It helped me not to think. I just repeated my secret mantra that was given to Sergei and me not so long ago. I had to cancel the exciting new TM classes that we wouldn't be able to attend together.

It seems very strange to me, but after six years of being in Israel, we didn't know much about Jewish rituals, not even about *Shiva*, the week-long period of mourning following burial where family members gather with visitors for prayers, comfort, and meals. Did we sit *Shiva* for Sergei? Perhaps, but I cannot remember.

The next morning, a thank-you letter came from Tel-Aviv for the present we had given at the wedding that we had recently attended. It was sent before the tragic day and had a beautiful picture of Sergei, Anechka and I with the newlyweds. We all looked young and happy. It was one of the last pictures that had been taken of Sergei. I put it on my nightstand, just to see his alive image, to have a visual connection. A few more pictures were developed later of the whole family at the new community pool, probably on August 17th. Smiling and cheerful Sergei having fun, swimming with the children, posing with us before the camera, enjoying the beautiful day.

I couldn't stop crying behind the closed doors...

I went to see Boris. I remember opening his door and seeing him sitting at the table alone, his sad eyes looking at me with such pain, love and understanding. No words were needed, I just came very close to him, hugged him, and stayed like this for a long, long time. Tears were in our eyes and grief in our hearts.

Eliezer came and graciously invited us to spend a week in their *kibbutz*. It was a timely and absolutely necessary bridge for us to cross to our new life without Sergei. Everyone, but mostly Menucha, was very attentive and sweet, and Eliezer hugged me lovingly and warmly, with compassion and understanding. Having my Mama by my side and the kids enjoying the nice *kibbutz* environment was a relief. Out of our apartment, breathing the fresh dry air, walking among the palm trees and even trying to help with some *kibbutz* chores, such as folding laundry at Menucha's clever suggestion, I started to come back to life little by little. Eliezer also tried to explain to me some of the Jewish customs –*Shiva*, *Shloshim* (30-day mourning period), what was allowed and what was not during the first year. It was very hard for me to relate to any of this, since I didn't want to move or to do anything at all.

Back home, it was much harder to adjust to reality. I began to lock all my feelings and memories deep inside for nobody to see, trying to protect my mother, Lala, and my children. I didn't give myself the permission to grieve as I should have. I had no idea about all those stages of grief that I would read about a few years later in America. We tried not to talk about the loss, and we didn't grieve as a family.

I wasn't sure if Yashenka understood what was happening and why his father had disappeared. I was afraid to mention the word *death*. A few days later as we were walking and I was holding his little hand, he asked me, "When is Abba coming back from the hospital?" My heart sank. I forced myself to say those horrible but simple words that were stuck in my throat,

"Yashenka, *solnyshco*, Abba is not coming home, because he was very sick and doctors couldn't save him, and Abba died." It felt like an electric shock had hit him as he abruptly pulled his hand from mine, stopped, looked at me in horror, and screamed,

"No, Ima, no!" and he started crying in the pain of understanding instinctively that his life had changed and his Abba would never be coming home again.

I think that my family and maybe others coming out of the inhumane Soviet society were doomed, lacking appropriate ways of dealing with unexpected turns in our personal lives. We struggled to invent our own inadequate coping mechanisms. Or maybe it was just me. I tried so hard to put on a happy face, to show strength, to keep my real feelings away from my children and my family, believing that it would help us to move on, to continue our journey.

The absence of God in our lives created such a void.

On the first of September, the beginning of the new school year, I went to work being so cheerful for my students, not even letting anybody know about my loss. I was proud of myself and my acting abilities.

But I was weeping quietly at night, lying in my empty bed without my Beloved at my side...

I would go to see Boris often and talk with him softly about life and death, unpredictability and senselessness, reconciliation and mercy. He showed such compassion toward me that my aching heart would melt a little. It was soothing and calming just to be with him. He would say also that it was so ironic for us to always worry so much about losing him, but instead we lost Sergei. Our questions about human faith had no answers for us. We just had to overcome.

A group of Sergei's coworkers came to visit the children and me at our apartment. I was surprised to see them and to hear all the compliments that they were expressing about the great character Sergei had, his kindness and the knowledge that he shared freely. Everyone was shocked by his untimely passing. Sergei was greatly loved and respected. I had never heard that from Sergei. He was very modest and didn't have a big ego. They told me that Sergei would be missed a lot. We never had friends among the Israelis, so this visit was very unusual for me to witness.

Shloshim arrived as a heavy moment for me. I wasn't ready to go back to the cemetery, but this time, I took Anat with me to be part of this Jewish ritual on the thirtieth day after his passing. She would be 10 years old in a week, and I thought she should go to say goodbye to her Abba. There were prayers, chanting and more prayers. Many people came to participate. I was hugging my sad daughter, looking at sad Tosca and my mother across from us. Endless sorrow! Everything was still a blur at this point, and I don't even remember when the headstone was erected.

The hardest thing for me was to live in the same place where everything reminded me endlessly of the absence of Sergei. The furniture, the books, the records, the pictures on the walls, the songs on the radio, the music, our car — everything that we had accumulated and shared together was there. It was all a constant reminder of Sergei's absence. Where was he? We had always eaten dinners together, and now there was an empty chair.

One day in a friend's apartment, I saw a book that Sergei had loaned to them to read. He had forgotten about it and had been looking for it for a long time. It was a book that he really liked and missed. As I was standing in the friend's apartment, suddenly I saw this book on their bookshelf, and I wanted to exclaim, "Here is your book, Sergei," nearly forgetting my reality.

It took a few long months for me to realize that the notion of 'Time is a healer' didn't apply to me, at least without drastically changing my circumstances. I had to figure out what changes I needed to make in order to survive and to start living again. I was only 34 years old and I was already barely alive inside.

I didn't have my Beloved to help me to make any decisions, to lead me. The time had come for me to take a stand. And, boy oh boy, did I surprise myself as well as everyone around me!

CHAPTER FORTY-THREE

Slowly, I started to formulate some ideas of how to save myself and keep my sanity, and to be able to continue living. I had to change the direction of my life, to find a new place where I could become whole again. I knew I would take Sergei with me on this new journey, but he would be hidden inside my soul and invisible to others.

The first time the thought came to me of going to America, it was unexpected and also a little scary. America? *Wow!!* I felt very excited thinking of this new adventure and new possibilities. But is it possible? How can someone just decide to move to America? Unlike in Russia, I had no idea about any guidelines, rules, or some known process to follow.

"Nobody just changes countries, like gloves," my mother would say later, overwhelmed by my crazy new idea.

I thought about my new plans often, without sharing my feelings with anyone. *What are the pros and cons? What do I have to offer? How would I make a living? I am just a good piano teacher but not the best around, even in Israel. I don't know the language. That's got to be the worst!! Am I losing my mind again? I have a sick father, my mother is getting older, I have two children to consider, as well as my sister's family. The only possible conclusion is that I am losing my mind. I have a great government job here in Israel with great benefits, I like my job and I am doing very well. I have a very good group of piano students. I make good money and can live here without any hardship. We all have our nice apartments, and my father has very good doctors. None of us has to pay for our medical care. I know nothing about America, even less than I knew about Israel at the beginning of our journey. I have Boris and Vera here. My conclusion — It would be insanity for me to even think about a second emigration and to move to America. I am losing my mind!!*

On the other hand, besides my strong personal reasons for leaving, I didn't like the direction that Israel was going. I was doubtful that there would ever be peace in this part of the world. I didn't want to live in insecurity surrounded by hateful enemies, and I was afraid for the future of my children. And my children were all that I had now. I had to bring them to the best country in the world and provide a better life for them. At least, I wouldn't be living under the socialistic system that Israel was in the process of adopting. I would open a new chapter for an exciting future! I would save my sanity by learning to exist without Sergei. *Can I do something crazy like this? On my own?*

I was going back and forth in my thoughts until one day I made a decision; I would go for a second emigration and fulfill Sergei's and my desire for a better life. At that moment I started talking with Mark, trying to convince him and explain to him my decision. My plan was to write to Eizer, who had lived in America for a few years by now and ask him his opinion. In the meantime, Mark was discussing it with Lala and then we were all talking with each other and with our parents. My sick father said right away, "Let's do it." And after a long conversation, we all agreed.

The letter came from Eizer. He said that Mark maybe would be able to find a job, because he has a Ph.D. in science and is a great specialist in his area of expertise. "But you, Ella, have absolutely zero chance to be able to stay in this country. The immigration laws are very strict and complicated," and he repeated, "Sorry, my dear, I wish I would be able to assist and help you, but with zero chance I don't think you should even try. Come for a visit and you would have a great trip. I would love to have you here, but please, don't be delusional."

My reaction right away was, *Eizer is one of my best friends, he would never steer me wrong. We followed him to Israel, and he is absolutely right. I have zero chance. And I will take it!! I will take this zero chance and I will go to America!!*

That was an incredible challenge, and I felt my blood rushing through me with enthusiasm and excitement. I had no more doubts, and I believed that if I really wanted it, somehow I would succeed.

We wrote a letter to Harold asking him if we could come for a visit. I didn't want to uncover our real plan and scare him right away; we didn't want him to discourage us from coming. I just wanted to be sure that Mark and I would have a place to stay at the beginning of our endeavor. While nervously waiting for a reply, I formed our plan: Mark and I would fly to New York in the summer months, when I would have a three-month paid vacation from the schools where I worked. Mark would take a vacation time and a leave of absence. We would spend the summer in America and figure out a way to emigrate and to bring the whole family there. Meanwhile, Mother and Lala would stay home and take care of my sick father and the children. Everybody agreed with the plan.

The letter came from Harold inviting us to come for a visit. *Wow!* Now it all started to become a reality and we had to plan accordingly to be ready to leave in a few months.

I went to Boris to tell him about my outrageous plan. I think he was shocked at first and with a sad, but strangely happy smile he said, "Are you stepping into the role of the Moses of the family now?" But he saw me alive again after many long months. At least I wanted something from life again. He had been worried about me for all this time and didn't have a solution for how to revive me. We both also had the mutual feeling of separation anxiety. We knew we would never see each other again, if I succeeded. I hugged him, thinking that life is so twisted and unexpected, many sided and unpredictable, sad, but happy, such a mix!

Boris was losing more of his muscles, and Vera had to help him with more and more tasks. I knew that we would miss each other a lot, and I wished that nothing like this would ever happen at all. But Boris understood me and thought I should at least try.

A few times, I went to the cemetery to talk to Sergei, telling him about my off-the-wall plan, hoping for his support. I let myself weep out loud, releasing my heartfelt emotions without anybody around. Touching the warm stone and reading Sergei's name in Hebrew was surreal, and it was hard for me to separate and leave. I knew that half of my heart would be left in this part of the world forever, no matter where the other part would be. I knew that without my Beloved, the planet Earth would always be empty for me in so many ways. But in some strange ways, Sergei had been helping me for a long time to be prepared for fulfilling the plans that I had in my head.

∞

Mark and I went to Tel-Aviv to get our visas. We were planning to become *Yordim*, a very small group of Israelis who wanted to leave the country. This move had a negative reaction from other Israelis at the time. Later, many Israelis moved to America and other countries, but at our time, it was still considered to be very shameful.

Finally, we bought our tickets for June 24, 1980. Once again, I was leaving my family behind, not knowing what would happen to us and what would happen to them. The situation with Lebanon was becoming progressively worse, and another war was on the horizon.

I was leaving my little children without either parent, not knowing for how long we would be apart, while I was supposedly going on a vacation with Mark. I never explained to them my plans to relocate to America. I was putting a lot of hard work on my mother's and my sister's shoulders. And I wasn't sure if I would see my father alive again.

Even now looking back, it seems very irrational and risky. At the end of the day, I had to turn my zero chance upside down into 100 percent for any success! Not realistic by any normal measures.

We said our goodbyes, took one suitcase for the two of us and left once again, but this time with some hope, not in tears. Everything inside me was alternating between sadness and excitement. "*I am leaving my children behind for a while*," but then,

"*I am going to America!!*"

I only can compare this feeling with perhaps the feelings of the astronauts, before they leave the Earth. The possibility of seeing America was as thrilling to me as a child going to Disneyland or Disneyworld for the first time. My anticipation of exploring the best country in the world and trying to understand its greatness was overwhelming.

My plan was to do everything we could to bring our children to America.

PART THREE

AMERICA

CHAPTER FORTY-FOUR

Harold greeted us at the airport, and right away, I felt a new and exciting energy all around me. I was in a different world, and *Americans* were everywhere! I had to pinch myself to be sure that I was not dreaming as we got into Harold's car and drove along city streets to his apartment. As I was thinking before my trip, New York actually was like a city on the moon. There was no way that it was on the same planet as other cities, especially one like Moscow! I felt so privileged to even come to America, when for millions people of the world it was absolutely impossible.

We drove through a small part of Greenwich Village around the University that seemed to me like a scene from a foreign movie. *Wow!* Young American students were all around, walking the tight streets; smiling, careless faces, casual clothes, hugging couples, the unknown-to-me energy of the non-worrying crowd. After a short drive, we came to the gorgeous and spacious apartment that Harold was occupying as a professor working at New York University.

The next morning, we had to uncover our plan, to the surprise of Harold. He had no idea how we could stay, or emigrate to this country. I think that he was shocked by this outrageous idea of ours and just politely covered up his panic inside. Then I showed to him our combined cash of about ten thousand dollars that we brought with us just in case we would succeed and would need cash to start our new lives. I knew that it wasn't that much money, but maybe it would be enough to begin with. Harold turned pale looking at the cash, and I had no idea why he seemed to be so overwhelmed.

"What should we do with this money, since apparently we can't carry it around?" I asked innocently. He was kind of gulping for air without saying a word to me. I was waiting for his suggestion and saw him getting more and more perplexed.

"You think it is not enough money to start out with? We have more at home, Harold; this is not our last dollar. We just didn't bring it all right away. Don't worry, we would never ask you for money. Why are you so worried?" Then he finally spoke and told me that he never saw so much cash in his life. Now I was perplexed!

"But, Harold, it's only ten thousand dollars!" I was a little confused, and so was Harold.

Well, he explained to us that apparently, Americans don't carry much cash at all. They use credit cards and checks from the bank instead. But now, somehow, he would have to explain to his banker the whole story about this sudden cash. He felt very uncomfortable. We went to the very stuffy bank, and Harold went to talk with the manager to explain the situation. Later, they invited me to the office, and the manager told me that if I would agree, he would open the account in my name, and I could make a deposit. One little detail: I needed to have a social security number, and if I would agree, he would get it for me. *Wow!!* I didn't know what it was, but it sounded very important. I looked at Harold, and he nodded his head "yes," and later explained to me how important this number is. I felt a little bit like an American, having my SSN and my bank account! *Wow!!*

Not long ago, I found a copy of a letter that I wrote to Boris and Vera ten days after my arrival in New York. This is a fascinating letter to read today, even for me. Here are a few lines:

> "Harold's apartment is on the 26th floor with more floors above it. *Wow!* The 4-way view opens the whole panorama of Manhattan with the Empire State Building in the center and a magnificent ensemble of 'smaller high-rises.' *Wow!* I can't believe my eyes not only with delight, but more so with surprise — New York always was such an unattainable, remote, and frightening place, and suddenly it is all alive, moving, multicolored, and populous — till your eyes are hurting...
>
> There is a completely different world that has nothing in common with the world that we knew in Russia and in Israel.

People are different. Everybody is dressed up 'to kill,' like they all are stars in a Hollywood movie, glossy, free in their expressions, very rich. I looked at them like they are all from a different planet, maybe from 'Mars,' and I am not sure what planet I am from.

Our Russian perception of the horrific endless crime here is a great Soviet propaganda and very exaggerated. So far, I haven't seen any police or the crime scenes. That didn't mean that in this huge city there is no crime, I am not that naïve, but even in Leningrad, we were afraid to go to certain areas. For example, Mark and I went through Union Square yesterday, and it was very strange for us because there were only black people looking suspiciously at us there and no white people — it felt as though we were invading their turf, and it was very uncomfortable! So now we know to go around Union Square.

But it is nothing like the image of this 'scared American' shaking from fear, sitting at home with all the doors locked, watching his colored television and being afraid of every noise around him. This is complete baloney!

And the subways are not the dirtiest and scariest place on Earth, as we always thought. Sure, they are nothing like Leningrad's palaces that the Soviets built under the ground to show off their greatness, but it is an efficient way for public transportation and serves the purpose.

Boris, America doesn't look like the weak country that we always thought it was. I think that Carter was a weak president, at least from our point of view. But the country is up for re-election in November, so change is in the air and there is hope for a much stronger government with much better leadership. There is a huge difference in the real world of freedom in this country, compared to the ugly world of our past.

I am listening to Harold, and with Mark's help trying to understand everything at once — hungry for new information and comprehension. Harold told us about all kind of movements and freedom of expression and disagreements between different groups of people. They are alive, strong in their convictions, and allowed to speak freely without fear. *Wow!!* Now I understand better why you always wanted to go to America — it seems to be the most fascinating and amazing country and I wish Sergei and I would have come here for a visit first, even before France. I am full of gratitude to be able to come here for this once-in-a-lifetime experience."

CHAPTER FORTY-FIVE

It was wonderful to be Harold's guests. He was such a gracious host. He actually gave up his bedroom for me, and offered the couch in his office for Mark. He slept in the living room on this narrow Army surplus cot that he put up every night. I am absolutely puzzled now, looking back — what was wrong with us to agree with such an outrageous arrangement? Definitely something was just lacking in our perceptions of what was appropriate. Every time I remember it, I feel awful and ashamed.

Harold's sister Annie came to greet us right away. After lunch she took us to Macy's to shop for a few necessities. I was choosing jeans to buy since they were so much cheaper than in Israel. I was holding my purse closed, as I usually do. But at the bus station, I opened my purse and didn't see my wallet. It was gone, and I panicked. I had more than $500 in cash in the wallet, which was a lot of money for me. But more importantly, it contained all my important papers, passport, and documents, and I was ready to cry like a little girl. Annie was visibly upset, mostly with herself, and Harold gave her a really bad time. "They are just so naïve," he was whispering to her when we came back. "You should warn them about the thievery in the city to prevent this unnecessary hardship."

But the most fascinating thing happened when Annie told me that tomorrow we would get my wallet back with everything there, except the cash. *What?* As hard as it was for me to believe, that is exactly what happened the next morning when my wallet, with everything in it minus the cash, was returned to me. It blew me away. What considerate thieves there are in this country, full of understanding and even kindness. *Wow!!*

Harold was a known expert psychologist who conducted many clinical trials in the area of stress and anxiety, working with his students at NYU. I had no idea back then what his field of work was all about. It had never occurred to us to protect ourselves from stress or trying to understand or analyze our anxieties. It was almost laughable to us that people would have the time and money to spend on this nonsense. Our lives were always about survival. But I had a lot of respect for Harold with the full understanding that there are so many new things that I have no idea about. The more I learned, the more I realized how little I knew.

Every night, Harold would invite us to a different restaurant for dinner and would never let us treat him. I had never eaten in restaurants in my entire life, except a very few times for very special occasions, but every night? The waitresses would always greet Harold, "Hello, professor," and then we would have the best meals in typical New York restaurants full of charm and ambiance. *Wow!!* We would go for lunch with Annie and Harold to ethnic places, and for the first time, we tried exotic and delicious Chinese food. *Wow!!* Who knew?

Mark and I were walking the streets of New York until late hours, absolutely enchanted. And it was a pre-Mayor Giuliani city — not very clean, and some parts were really dangerous according to Harold — nothing like the safe and beautiful city it is today. I felt drunk without any alcohol, just looking around and watching the busy people of Manhattan, who displayed such confidence, joyfulness, and high self-esteem (the term that had no place in our previous life or doesn't even have a good translation into the Russian language). I couldn't relate to those people, had no idea of what their inner world was like, what was their life all about. Did they even have any problems in their life? What makes them tick, what makes them laugh or cry, who are they afraid of, what do they like? Do they really feel happy in their lives, or are they just wearing a mask of happiness? I never encountered such polite people in my life — smiles everywhere, courtesy, and a readiness to help a stranger.

We entered the deli for lunch for the first time without Harold. So many choices! How do they know what to order? We watched the line moving along, and smiling servers asked some questions and people replied, and in a few minutes, they would get huge sandwiches and some drinks in a cup or bottle. I felt so inadequate, unprepared, and embarrassed like a little kid, while Mark tried to explain our order to the smiley girl with the help of a few words and gestures of complete confusion. To our surprise the girl didn't stop smiling and tried to be as helpful as possible. "What planet are we on?" I asked Mark. Throughout our lives, we had experienced of rudeness and disrespectfulness from bad-mannered salespeople in the U.S.S.R.

The architecture of Manhattan simply blew my mind away. Looking up to see high-rises, I felt an overwhelming sense of wonder and splendor. It seemed to me to be some kind of symbol of American greatness and achievements of unearthly proportions.

The "millions" of stores with artistic window displays looked very inviting, but not to me. I wasn't brave enough to enter the stores and face the sales people, knowing that I can't afford to buy anything anyway. But window shopping was an amazing experience by itself. Luxury, elegance, wealth…"Mama, Mia!" Endless rows of fancy restaurants with "millions" of different cuisines. *People are living in the Garden of Eden here!*I thought. *Do they even know it, or understand it?*

Theaters of Broadway! I had heard about them in my past life, but now seeing this with my own eyes was unreal. I wanted to go and see all the shows and concerts. We were standing with Mark in front of a theater showing the musical *Calcutta* and we debated back and forth if we could afford $20 tickets. Unfortunately, and despite having such a strong desire to enter the theater and see the show, we decided against it. I was like a hungry cat watching a mouse from behind a window.

After a couple of weeks of euphoria, we needed to accomplish our mission and start figuring out how to be able to stay in this blessed country. We had our visitors' visas that would expire in three months. Our time was limited, and we had no great ideas. Harold contacted a lot of his friends, but nobody really had any suggestions. Mark sent his résumés to many places and Harold drove him for his interviews, taking me along for a ride. Companies were very interested, but not without the *Green Card*.

Oh, this name *Green Card* became the magic key that would unlock everything. Walking the streets and seeing all kinds of people moving along, I felt so disadvantaged. *All of them have the right to live here and enjoy their simple lives, except us,* I was thinking with real jealousy and sadness.

Harold made a professional résumé for me, but I didn't even know where to send it. He was impressed with my knowledge of Eurhythmic and suggested I talk to somebody from Julliard, but with my limited English and inability to understand the answers, I felt very inadequate. We went to visit a few of his friends working in the high rises and finally saw those American bosses with cigars and their feet on the desks. *Wow!!* They were all sympathetic, but nothing more than that.

We went to the Jewish Community Center (JCC) to discuss our intentions, but they didn't even let us into the room to talk. We were absolutely rejected. Israelis, even from Russia, should live in Israel. *Period.* I remembered Arlette's reaction in Paris. Do American Jews also have this same attitude toward other Jews?

Time was going fast. We tried to write optimistic letters home with our updates, but unfortunately, we had nothing to brag about. It was very worrisome and unsettling.

We went to visit our friend Eizer in Philadelphia. Nice home, American lifestyle, two cars. *Wow!!* It was great to see him and his family again, but with sadness, he told us again that he still believed that I realistically have the same zero chance to get a *Green Card,* and he wished he had some power to help us. We had a good time with Eizer, but Mark's mood started to become sour on the way back to New York.

What chance did we have?

I still felt that this was not the end, and somehow, something would come up. We felt that we were overstaying Harold's hospitality, big time. Finally, with the help of some Russian friends, we moved to a small apartment in Brooklyn — a very different experience than to live in Manhattan. Mark continued to send his résumés all over the country, with no luck. I didn't know where to send my résumés and was wracking my brain, thinking, *What else can I do?*

It was a hot and humid August in New York. We decided to give ourselves a time limit until the end of the month. If nothing breaks through, we will return home, and at least we could say that we tried. My optimism was still with me despite our very poor prognosis.

And then Mark decided to go to California to visit his brother, whose entire family had been lucky enough to come straight from Russia to America. At least, if nothing else, one goal would be accomplished — to see the family.

CHAPTER FORTY-SIX

I had briefly met Mark's brother Izia and his wife Raya in Leningrad. Back then, I heard the tragic story of Mark's family during the war.

Mordechai and Miriam, Mark's parents, were soul mates and had a blissful family before the beginning of the war. They belonged to a huge Jewish family of brothers, sisters, uncles, aunts, and many cousins, who slowly but steadily moved to Leningrad from the shtetls of Belorussia. They were a very religious family and continued their Jewish traditions, no matter what. Mordechai was a prominent member of the only synagogue in the city of Leningrad. Their lives were similar to the story of Simon Korobochko, and perhaps they even knew each other back then, since it was a rare situation to continue to be a religious Jew in Stalin's Leningrad. Mordechai was a central part of the whole *mishpucha* (family) and the most devoted, committed to following all the laws of the Torah. His wife Miriam adored him and was his better half for life. By the time this unexpected war ruined their lives, they had three children: an older daughter, and two sons, Izia and Mark. Mark was the youngest, only three years old.

As with most people in the Soviet Union, their contented life dramatically and abruptly changed in the middle of June, 1941. Mordechai was mobilized into the Red Army and was sent to defend Leningrad. Like my father, he was wounded in the fierce battles to protect his city, and was sent to the hospital. Besides dealing with his critical wounds, he also was very suspicious of the terrible food in the hospital, since all his life he had eaten only kosher food. Unfortunately, he did not survive, despite his strong desire to live for his wife and children.

It was a terrible tragedy for Miriam, and for the whole family. Mordechai's death devastated his wife, who was extremely attached to him, loved him completely, and was dependent on him all through their marriage. Her grief was unbearable. When these difficult times pushed her to the limit, she felt numb and detached from reality. Living in the blockade of Leningrad without her husband and caring for three children was more than she could bear. Miriam didn't have the strength to survive under these dreadful circumstances. She gave her portions of bread to her children and started losing strength very rapidly. Depression was wearing her down, malnutrition destroyed her health, and she couldn't fight the horror of her surroundings. Miriam passed away just one month after her husband.

Their children were suddenly orphans with no place to go. Thankfully, some relatives took the boys' older sister under their care, but the two little brothers were sent to separate orphanages in two different areas of Russia. The only episode from his early childhood that Mark remembered was the exciting moment of his evacuation from the blockade of Leningrad on a boat through Lake Ladoga.

Apparently, the German airplanes were bombing all moving objects with precision, and succeeded in striking the boat full of orphaned children, which ignited a fire and started a panic among the adults who were escorting the minors. Luckily, another boat was heading in the same direction and when it moved closer to the burning boat, all of the adults lined up and started tossing the children from one adult to another and from one boat to the next, as the fire was raging, ready to burn everything and everybody.

That was the moment that Mark has remembered all his life as the most exciting and thrilling episode of his childhood. He loved being thrown from one person to another, and when he landed safely on the new boat he begged the last person to throw him back like that again and again, back and forth. And the picture of this "fire of death" in the middle of the night was an electrifying and exhilarating memory that has never left Mark to this day.

Eventually, three-year-old Mark found himself in the middle of Russia in a small village, where he was the only Jewish boy in memory. He had been illegally circumcised under his father's supervision, and that made him very unique in this orphanage, full of Russian children who were ready to fight with him and each other for any reason. The boys were real hooligans, growing up in this rough atmosphere with minimum care from the overwhelmed stuff, scarce food, with not much warmth or expressions of love from the overtired and overworked employees. Mark told me that he became a fierce fighter, almost animalistic and ruthless, with no fear and no mercy. He would do anything to win, even over the older boys, until everyone was afraid to even touch him. In this way, he earned their respect, and they left him alone. That was his survival mechanism.

Knowing Mark, it is impossible to imagine him being this kind of wild child; it is so much out of his character. He has a very soft demeanor, with inherent politeness and kindness. But he remembers vividly many wild episodes that he took part in during those formative years of his orphaned upbringing.

To survive, Mark also learned how to steal anything edible from the neighboring farms or fruit gardens and to run away as fast as possible, so that he would not be caught by the angry owners. At age five, he learned to smoke cigarettes from the older children, and he taught himself to swim by jumping into the local river by himself, without any instruction.

He happened to be an exceptionally smart and intelligent boy, though, and was by far the best student in math and science. Mark had an astonishing capacity to memorize and remember, and an unusual curiosity. But most of all, he loved to read all kind of books from a very young age, and all through his school years. Boys asked him to read adventure books out loud before going to sleep, and that became their ritual.

There were a few excellent teachers in this orphanage since most of them were not allowed to go back home to Leningrad or Moscow after their sentences in Stalin's camps were over. They were forced to live in the periphery. Their unfortunate situation was a blessing for Mark, and he took full advantage of this circumstance to advance rapidly in his studies.

Mark didn't remember much about his family at all and grew up as a kid without a past history, except for his non-Russian last name and non-Russian looks. The orphanage was the only family he ever knew or remembered, and he tried to survive as best as he could. He never had any curiosity, though, about his real family. He didn't try to find his relatives, even when he became older. But they had been looking for him for many years, and one day, a cousin of his arrived at the orphanage. The cousin explained Mark's family history to him, and wanted to take him back to Leningrad. Mark didn't want to go. He was at home, didn't feel deprived of anything, didn't know much about the outside world, and refused to leave the orphanage.

He was only sixteen years old when he graduated from high school. The idea of moving to Leningrad at that time became very attractive since he wanted to get a higher education. After an emotional separation from his orphanage family, he set out upon this new adventure.

I can only imagine the arrival of Mark, Mordechai's son, in Leningrad. The whole *mishpucha* had been waiting for this moment for more than ten years. For the first time since young childhood, he met his sister and his brother, whom he obviously didn't remember. There were hugs, kisses, and endless introductions of many new relatives, laughter, jumps of joy, tears, and emotional outbursts. Mark didn't expect any of this. He was overwhelmed, pretty much detached, and almost annoyed. His emotional development had suffered for so many years that it was hard for him to react positively to this new family, who were freely showing their love and affection for him. He entered the new world and had a hard time relating to this unknown environment. When one of his aunts, who came later, tried to introduce herself, he had had enough of this "craziness" and angrily replied, "No more aunts, no more relatives. I've had enough already, and I don't want any more!"

It took a while for Mark to get used to this new life with a new family in a new city. Eventually, he became very close to this Jewish family of his, learned about many traditions and holidays, and thought that most Jews lived like that, until he met my sister many years later and realized the big difference between his *mishpucha* and our non-religious family. But it was only through falling in love and marrying my beautiful sister Lala that Mark started to feel a real sense of the meaning of *family*. He loved our parents, experiencing their unique warmth, connection, care and devotion. He called them Mama and Papa for the first time in his life, after not having parents for nearly 30 years. We all created very close ties between us on our journey through the complicated roads of our lives.

The paradox though, was that all those religious families didn't pioneer the exodus to Israel, and even opposed it, but our non-religious family did. And Mark's example was later followed by many of his relatives, who eventually left Russia for Israel and America.

In the meantime, right after coming to Leningrad, Mark entered the university and graduated as an electrical engineer and later, just before our ordeal with Israel, got his Ph.D. Eventually, while working in Israel and later in America, he became one of the leading experts in the world in the area of lightning protection. Mark and Lala traveled the world together as Mark took part in international conferences and symposiums, giving lectures on this crucial subject, being a guest of honor, and deserving the respect of many of his colleagues.

But our future story would never have happened if we hadn't decided to take a trip to California to see Mark's brother and his family. This trip changed our lives and the history of our entire family.

CHAPTER FORTY-SEVEN

California...

My first impression of San Jose was mixed. After the excitement of New York, everything seemed to be more ordinary and unappealing. It reminded me of a documentary shown in the U.S.S.R. called *One Floor America*, with beautiful weather and nature on one hand, and old ugly houses on the other. The casual, almost sloppy way of dressing in California really surprised me, seeing all those Bermuda shorts and sports shirts.

There was a big community of Russian Jews in San Jose that had emigrated as a second wave after us. They came directly to the U.S.A. from Russia. I listened to them in amazement. They didn't have our grueling experience leaving the U.S.S.R., didn't know anything about Israel, didn't go through the war and after-war tribulations. They had a smooth ride into sunny California, where they were greeted with honors and received a lot of real help from the local Jewish community and individual rich Jews. But no one in the Jewish community would help us, even with suggestions. They didn't even want to talk to us, shutting the door in our face, or would ignore us completely. Those who came straight from Russia, however, were their heroes.

A big crowd, mostly people from Leningrad, came to a party held at Mark's brother Izia's apartment to meet and to greet us. They wanted to learn about Israel and about our life there. We were ready to share with them our experience, but after our introduction and a few words, the discussion went into complete disarray. They started arguing about their own ideas and understanding of all kind of problems in Israel, America, and Russia, complications with immigration and the unfairness of their own life's struggles, and on and on and on. I got lost listening to them, but I loved the people immediately. They were my kind of Leningraders that I had missed all those years. I only had Boris and Vera in Israel as real, close friends and I wished Boris and Vera were here in Palo Alto rather than sitting by themselves in Kiryat Yam.

I became friends with many of them instantly. It's like I had known them for many, many years before. Their history was the same as mine. They had the same outlook on life, the same background, and the same experiences in the past. It was a closeness born of the experiences we had shared, of acceptance and deep understanding of each other. We didn't need a lot of words to communicate, and I knew that they "felt my pain" right away. They were helping each other in all possible ways, but no one had any idea how to help us.

I missed New York and had a hard time understanding the California suburbs. All my friends bought old clunky cars. No adequate transportation was available, and there were no people walking on the streets. Very strange... people drove cars everywhere, even to the local grocery store. And then I discovered the Supermarket. My friend Lena invited me to go shopping with her and I entered Safeway unprepared —*Wow!* It was impossible for me to imagine, this display of indulgence and over-the-top displays of more and more endless indulgence! I was lost... *Is it ever possible to try all those beautifully wrapped products in all their varieties? How can people choose what to buy?* The size of the store was tremendous. *Is there some map, a guide to navigate the store?* The fruits and vegetables displays looked like so picture-perfect, it was hard to believe that they were real. There were many things I had never seen in my life. For example, *broccoli—what is this?*

We entered the "pet" aisle. I became very uncomfortable, shaking my head, almost crying, *Why, why would they have so many different foods and toys just for dogs and cats? People are starving in so many places in the world! We had to stand in lines for hours just to get any almost inedible food in Russia. My sister and I never had any toys growing up. But here, even a dog was treated like a king!* Something so unjust and unfair was happening in this world. It was hard to comprehend... People were piling and piling more and more food into their carts, up to the hilt. I wondered, *How much food does one family eat in the USA?* Unbelievable...

We never had a refrigerator while I was growing up in Russia, so we would walk to the *Gastronome* store every day, buying the same food — no assortment, no variety — the same bread, bologna, cheese and butter, maybe eggs, and some potatoes, carrots, onions and cabbage. And that's on a good day! In Israel we had plenty of great produce, but in small *makolets*, or food shops. The Safeway in San Jose apparently was just one of many supermarkets in the area and not the best one, as Lena explained to me later. There were much better and fancier ones around. Really?

We were staying in the center of Silicon Valley, a booming area for technological industries, the hub of innovative electronic and computer companies. Most of my new friends became part of the new technological revolution that was taking place throughout the world. I started to doubt my decision to listen to my father in choosing my profession. *If I would only have finished technical college, I would be able to be part of the "happening crowd" and could have found a job much easier, even without a Green Card. I could have found my place under the American sun, but not with my great profession of teaching piano...*

Time went on quickly with us trying to find a solution for finding jobs, with no results. Mark was losing his optimism very rapidly, and so was I, maybe just a little more slowly. In reality, nothing worked for us, and it was time to make our preparation to go back home and to buy our airline tickets. We knew also that it was getting harder for our family at home to be without us for so long without any promising news.

My brilliant plan was just an illusion, wishful thinking. I had to come to terms with our complete failure and with heavy sadness creeping into my heart, I was preparing myself to talk to Mark about going back home. At least we had tried, and we saw beautiful America. Plus, we got to spend time with Harold and Annie, we visited Eizer and made some new friends. I was ready to pick up the pieces and go back to Israel. But my intuition and the hope of a successful mission was still alive in me.

What happened next was a pivotal moment for my family and me.

CHAPTER FORTY-EIGHT

I met Edidia, an Israeli guy working as a real estate agent for one of my friends, and we had a long conversation about life in Israel vs. life in America, back and forth. During the conversation he mentioned that his wife Shoshana was working as a teacher in the local Jewish school. He gave me her telephone number just in case I would like to get some more information. A Jewish school? Not a music school?

Wait a second, Ellochka, I thought, *You worked in the school district in Israel, and, thanks to Sergei, you are a Eurhythmic specialist, aren't you? Sergei insisted that you take this special course, remember? Maybe they can use you in this capacity?*

My heart was jumping up and down in some kind of dance of its own, and my head was jumping from one thought to another. Suddenly, the light bulb turned on in my head like lightning — a Jewish-American school, *Wow!!* I hadn't even thought about this obvious venue. There may be some possibilities here! I must go to this school tomorrow, forget calling the wife of this messenger, just go...

I couldn't sleep that night, thinking about how I could present myself with my very limited English to the American principal of this American-Jewish school. They probably would want me to go back to Israel, like all the other Jewish organizations did. How should I tell them that I don't even have a *Green Card*, so I really can't work in the USA? Why would they even want to listen to me? Should I mention Sergei and hope for some understanding? What else could I say to make my case to some stranger in this strange country?

I opened the door at the office of the Jewish school the next morning and saw a receptionist looking straight at me with a questioning face. "How can I help you?" I wasn't sure who she was and didn't know if she could help me. *Who do I want to see? Maybe, the director of the pre-school?* As I was thinking how to answer her, I saw a woman with short gray hair standing behind the receptionist and looking out the window. She turned around, looked straight at me with her blue eyes, our eyes met and we connected immediately. I don't know how to describe it, but I had an unusual feeling all through me of some kind of recognition, like we knew each other from before, like a meeting of our souls or something like that. It was like she understood right there all about Elvira, which was my full name. I looked so indecisive, so lost, and so tongue-tied.

She introduced herself as "Joyce, Joyce Wertman" and extended her hand, smiling at me. I started feeling much better right away. "Come with me to my office, Mrs. Okun," she said after I introduced myself. "What brought you to our school this morning?" she asked. I took a deep breath, thinking that this was my chance to tell her something extraordinary to impress this lovely woman once and for all. "Are you from Russia?" she asked. "My father came to this country from Russia a very long time ago and I hold his memory very close to my heart. Anyway, are you looking for a place to enroll your children here?"

I felt much more comfortable now to tell her in my broken English that I am actually looking for a job. I showed her my beautiful résumé that Harold wrote for me. She read it very intensely. "Oh, you lived and worked in Israel? I know a little bit about Eurhythmic — it's a great program for young children. What about your family, are you here alone?" I tried my best to put a few words together to describe to her my situation and my desire to move to America.

"Well," said Joyce, "as strange as it sounds, I actually desperately need an assistant teacher in the classroom for the three-year-olds. I haven't found a good one so far, and today is already the seventh of September. I also have some Russian and Hebrew-speaking students, but most of my teachers speak only English. I would like to see you working with our students right now. Would you follow me to the classroom, please?"

We entered the room, and I saw about fifteen busy little children in a big light room full of colorful toys and their teacher helping them with some projects at a little table. I had never worked with little ones and had no idea what to do. Joyce nodded to the teacher and they started to talk in the corner of the room, watching me. *My, God! What should I do? My life depends on this presentation and I don't quite understand what I should reveal to Joyce: what is her expectation??*

Just then, a beautiful little blonde angel girl named Ava came close to me, took me by my hand, and started asking something in English and I had no idea what she was saying, but I lowered myself to my knees down to her level and was trying in vain to understand at least a couple of words. Meanwhile, some other children came along, and Ava pulled me by my hand, leading me to the table to show me her art — bright colors and a lot of glitter. I smiled and started helping her to decorate the picture using different crayons and felt so thankful to this sweet angel. Then I heard some Hebrew being spoken and started conversing with and helping the Israeli kids, and got really involved in their tasks. For a few minutes I almost forgot about Joyce and Sherry, the classroom teacher, who were both watching me all that time from the corner of the room. I don't know how long their observation lasted, but after a while, Joyce told me to say goodbye to the kids and Sherry, and brought me back to her office.

"I love the way you interacted with the children," she said. "I was looking for a teacher with your specific qualifications all summer long and couldn't find one. So far, we have started the year without the second teacher in this room. I think we can work together and incorporate your music program into our schedule and your Russian and Hebrew into our system. I am so happy, that you came today. It solves our desperate situation. Many of our parents will be very pleased."

I couldn't believe my ears. Is this really happening? Did I understand Joyce's English correctly?

Wait a second. "Joyce, but I forgot to tell you the most important thing— I don't have a *Green Card*. With all the excitement, I didn't even mention to her my enormous and unsolvable problem. This could put an end to it all. How in the world would she be able to deal with my apparently unsolvable problem? Achieving my goal was achingly close, so possible. I was ready to cry when I heard her calm response: "I have to get more information about the procedure and talk to the rabbi who is the principal of the school. I'll show him your very impressive résumé and credentials and we'll figure it all out, Elvira, don't worry. Meantime, I would like you to come to work tomorrow at 8 o'clock in the morning. Welcome aboard!" She smiled warmly, like an angel, and said goodbye to me, leading me to the door.

∞

Wow! Wow!! Wow!!!

I was standing in the middle of the playground looking at all the cheerful noisy children running around, playing, swinging, and biking. *Wait a second, what just happened a few minutes ago? Am I dreaming?? Is this really happening? Did I really get the job? Does this mean I can stay and work here, eventually get a Green Card and bring my children, whom I miss so much, to America?? But what about Mark now? It's getting even more complicated — what should Mark do? I got a job but he didn't? Eizer was wrong with his predictions; it is all upside down – I GOT A JOB!!! But it doesn't make things easier for us.*

Flying high up in the clouds and feeling down at the same time, I hurried to talk with Mark to tell him my astonishing news. He was obviously so incredibly ecstatic and also surprised by the turn of events. *Wow!!* We celebrated with some of our new friends and everyone congratulated me on this huge victory of my spirit. I called Harold to tell him my story and he was *so* thrilled, and conveyed to me his admiration for my determination and strength in achieving my goals.

"You are an extremely resilient girl, Ella. Heartfelt congratulations and *Mazel Tov* from me and Annie." I thanked him and later looked up the word **resilient** in the dictionary.

Writing a long letter home, I revealed to my children and my family my incredible and unbelievable news. What about Mark? I believed that somehow, he would follow me to success, too. There was no other possibility. Now it was his turn to succeed. Mark decided to go back to New York by himself and with more resolve than ever to continue his search for the special position that would need his qualifications. He left soon after I started my new job in the U.S.A.

I loved my new job — the children, the teachers, the Jewish education that I was receiving along with the students for the first time in my life, the prayers and chants that I was learning with the little ones. In many ways I was on their level, but in English, I was on a lower level than the three-year-olds. There were a lot of Israeli children and a few Russians and my knowledge of those languages and my music skills were very helpful and needed. I even picked up the accordion and taught myself to play it for the assemblies and holidays that were celebrated outdoors.

Joyce was my savior, my angel, my guardian, my teacher and mentor, my friend. No one else in my entire life had played such a pivotal role as Joyce. She helped me through so many difficult times with such incredible compassion and willingness to do everything, both possible and impossible, to assist my family and me. She went all the way to do everything needed to set me up with the immigration lawyer, getting all the complicated documentation and papers ready. She was very supportive during many months of uncertainty and struggles to get the rarely used special H1 immigration visa that was given only to people who possessed outstanding skills for certain types of work where equivalent skills among Americans could not be found. During all those months and months of the visa waiting period, Joyce was right by my side, optimistic and encouraging.

CHAPTER FORTY-NINE

J oyce introduced me to her family, and I felt at ease with all of them. It felt as if they were my American family that I had never known. Joyce's married life was very blissful, and it stood out among all the couples I have ever known on this planet. Joyce and Chuck were in love all their lives from the first day they met to the last, when Chuck passed away many years later. I witnessed this exceptional marriage for many years and understood that in very rare instances, it's actually possible, as an exception to the general rule. I felt so grateful to see it with my own eyes and not just read about it in some novel. I always thought that my marriage to Sergei was very remarkable too, but it was cut so short. I had tried to convince myself that perfection just cannot sustain itself on this planet, that the fairy tales could survive only for a short while, that our souls need more hardship to learn more lessons from more complicated relationships. Otherwise, how else could I explain Sergei's disappearance? But for Joyce and Chuck, this perfection lasted a lifetime. *Wow!!*

Meanwhile, I had the hospitable family of Mark's brother Izia and his wife Raya, who were helping me to survive. Raya's parents graciously let me sleep in their apartment, fed me after my work day and I had a supportive net all around me. I felt warmth and kindness in this otherwise very unusual situation, and I am forever grateful to them all.

My own mood was cautiously optimistic about the future of my family, but I missed my children so much, feeling so guilty leaving them without both parents for so long. In many quiet moments, I would let my guard down and let myself to be just a young sad widow who left her children so far away while waiting for a miracle in this new land. I wrote letters and called on the phone to talk with them, but phone calls were very expensive back then, and to hear their voices was such a delightful but heartbreaking experience. Just a little more than one year ago my own happy family life had been intact. How drastically things had changed in such a short time!

Anechka, Yashenka – would you ever understand my broken heart, my broken soul, and my broken dreams? Would you ever forgive me for leaving you without Abba and me for so long? How are you going to be affected by my actions? Am I even right to flee and try to change your lives so drastically? I didn't abandon you, my dearest ones. I just tried to do the best I could under very difficult circumstances! I cried quietly at night, but would get up in the morning and go to work with a smile.

The situation with Mark wasn't getting any better. After hundreds and hundreds of résumés that he had sent all over the U.S.A., he had received hundreds of rejections. Everyone was still interested in inviting him for an interview, but only after he had obtained his *Green Card* somehow. It was November by this time, and Mark was losing his optimism faster and faster. It was hard for him to live by himself, without his family and me for support in his small apartment in Brooklyn, and his leave of absence in Israel was coming to an end. He didn't want to lose his job in Israel. I tried to assure him that something positive would happen for him soon. I was talking on the phone with Mark very often, giving him all my support, but even I started to feel less and less optimistic. He gave himself a time limit to the end of November and wrote a letter to Lala describing his desperate situation.

I was so upset, thinking that my sister, who was the backbone of this whole operation, would get discouraged realizing that now, after all that we had been through, our families would be living so far apart in two different countries; this time by our own choice. I had such a deep appreciation for my sister and my parents for their help and support, for being our second front with full understanding that without them, our dream would not be realized. It was only through the combined effort of our entire family that we could achieve our desired success.

I didn't have peace of mind and started to have serious concerns about Mark's inability to get a job, and anxiety about being left alone in this new country if he went back home without me. I couldn't sleep, I couldn't eat, I couldn't meditate. I was losing my heart.

But God had his plan for Mark too — I just didn't know about it yet...

Mark called me one week before his deadline and with a changed, alive voice he told me that *finally*, some man had called him from Southern California and was very interested to see Mark for an interview. His name was Roy and he wanted to give Mark a chance to work for him and to help him get his *Green Card* !

Wow!! Wow!! Wow!!

The truth is that usually, things like that only happen in American movies that have happy endings. Statistically speaking, these were improbable events for both of us to find employment in our new country under the circumstances. But in our lives, it was a reality, a dream come true.

Sometimes, the heart can be broken from happiness, not only from sadness. I was just out of my mind after this conversation with Mark .The stress of the last fifteen months of my life that I had kept thoroughly inside myself just broke loose now, and I almost collapsed to the floor with some kind of pain all over my body with difficulty breathing and chattering teeth. Mark's brother Izia rushed me to the hospital, and after testing, the ER doctor gave me some tranquillizers and something else, and let me rest quietly for a long time with an IV in my arm, watching some monitors and measuring my blood pressure. I was lying in a hospital bed with a big smile on my face that even the pain couldn't erase.

Sergei, my Beloved, I did it — can you hear me? I want you to be proud of me. I want you to see that I am a resilient girl, like Harold said. I am a survivor. Even without you, I am with you, and you are with me, even though we are separated into two worlds. I have no idea about your world, but I feel your presence, and I feel that you are protecting us all and helping me to cope with life. I felt a lump in my throat, breathing became hard, and then tears slowly came over my heart and my soul, and I recognized that those were tears of deep sadness mixed together with the tears of unbelievable happiness.

My mission was accomplished for now...

Our first step was to get jobs. Now we had to wait for our lawyer to go through the system of the immigration jungle and see if it would be possible for us to get the temporary H1 visas that would eventually get us our *Green Cards*.

CHAPTER FIFTY

M onth after month, we were waiting for our fate to be decided by the immigration authorities. Mark was living in Southern California and working in a small lightning protection company, creating a device that would become one of the best in the world. His invention eventually would make his boss, the owner of the company, an extremely rich man. Roy, his boss, was paying a low salary to Mark for his innovative discoveries, but he agreed to work on Mark's *Green Card* and that was worth everything to us. We didn't know how long we would have to wait before the decision would be made, and so we patiently counted the days, living in limbo.

I wasn't interested yet and couldn't understand the politics of this country, but could feel a lot of tension between people after Reagan came into office. Some were so happy and hoping for change, including me, but a lot of Jewish people were very liberal and were upset about the elections — surprise, surprise! I figured out that in Russia and in Israel, most Jews were poor and wanted to fight for the betterment of society, for equality, and prosperity. In the U.S.A. many Jews were rich, but still wouldn't change their ideology no matter what. The same socialistic ideas that we encountered in Russia and Israel were preventing them from thinking clearly. It was very disappointing to me and I wrote about my findings to Boris in disbelief.

A few times, I was invited to parties and observed people with curiosity. My English was getting better after Joyce suggested that I read as many children's books as possible. I was now in an English-speaking environment, and having a "good ear," I started to pick up some typical phrases, words, and expressions. In any case, I was taken aback as to why the Americans didn't show any interest in knowing more about my life under communism in the Soviet Union. All of us had lived during the

Cold War. Yet almost no one showed any interest at all, except for some comments such as,

"How could you live in fear of speaking your mind freely? We would never accept this kind of oppression!" And then they were off to the next subject, or just making small talk. They seemed to be very gullible and naïve, but content and relaxed. There were not even many questions about life in Israel, although most of this generation of Jews loved and supported Israel at that time.

There was not much curiosity at all, or much patriotism about their great country. That was a huge surprise for me. I would proclaim to them that America was always a beacon of goodness and freedom for thinking people, the hope of the world, the best country ever created on this planet. Their reply would be,

"Really? Do you know how high our interest rate is now? 18 percent, outrageous! And our taxes? And the prices?"

"What? What are you talking about, my new friends? What a narrow vision you have! How can you complain about your splendid lives? What do you know or want to know about all those poverty-ridden countries, living under oppressive despots? How can you be so shallow?" I was trying to calm myself down and give myself a little more time to understand this country and its system.

Before long, winter came to an end, and spring was in the air. The teachers would bring all the students to play outside on the playground and talk a little bit while watching the children. One day I saw Joyce coming to the playground with a middle-aged lady at her side. They came close to us, and Joyce introduced her. "Please, welcome our new assistant teacher, Sara." I looked at Sara and saw her timid smile, insecurity and sweetness, and much more that I couldn't formulate for myself. There was something about her that was very intriguing, unusual, and extremely attractive to me, but I was taken aback by my own reaction to her.

The next day, we were talking nonstop while watching the children outside. She had grown up in Israel, but lived most of her life in the U.S.A. Finally, I could speak Hebrew and express myself as an adult, and it was a relief. She told me that she had been a homemaker most of her life, but her husband had passed away, and she had to start working again. She had three children close to my age, and a few grandchildren. Sara was quite insecure at work at the beginning and appreciated Joyce giving her a chance. I listened to her stories and ideas about life and was more and more intrigued. I felt that she had something important in her soul that I was lacking, but I had no idea what it was. My intuition told me, though…

Slowly I started to open up to her about my life in a way that I never had before. I could do it with Boris, but with a stranger? Nevertheless, I was waiting for the break time to go outside to assist the kids, but mostly to talk with Sara. She saw me suffering without my children and endlessly waiting for the results from my lawyer.

CHAPTER FIFTY-ONE

One morning Sara looked at me with her bright brown eyes and simply said,

"God has been watching over you and your family all this time, my dear Elvira. God is paving the way!" I looked straight back at her and very strongly and convincingly told her,

"Sara, I don't believe in God. What are you talking about?"

"Sure you believe in God, Elvira. You have believed in God all your life. You just don't know it yet!" I looked at her, dumfounded, with my eyes and mouth wide open, searching for an appropriate response.

I didn't know what to say to her, so sure and uncompromising was her statement. She smiled at me and calmly said, "Elohim has been with you all your life, has never left you, and never will." My head was working overtime trying to find the right words or concepts to tell Sara about how wrong she was, how old fashioned, how primitive and uneducated she sounded. But I was standing there quietly, forgetting even about my responsibility to watch the kids.

No one had ever talked to me like this; I had never heard those categorical words. *How does this woman know anything about my belief system? Why would she suddenly tell me in no uncertain terms something so strong that it turns my head upside down? Why am I listening to her? Why am I even talking to her? She thinks she knows more about me than I know about myself? What exactly is she trying to convey to me? Some bobe-mises, some nonsense?*

But why can't I answer her? Why does it actually and unexpectedly sound so TRUE to me??

What if she is right?

This is really scary!

Elohim? — It sounds so much better then God or Bog in Russian! Everything is spinning in my head...

Sara just looked at me calmly and let me digest these simple words of truth.

"Take your time, Elvira," she said to me as we were guiding the children back to the room for lunch.

The real truth was that I didn't have to take my time at all. I knew right then and there that she was right. I always knew it inside of me somewhere in my subconscious mind. Sara just gave me permission to believe and took a taboo off my shoulders. I would spend the rest of my life trying to find answers about religion and spirituality, but even my communist upbringing couldn't prevent me from believing what deep down inside I knew to be true. I would never be a robot again, a product of the Soviet system. Enough is enough!

I reflected on my life and our pragmatic atheistic approach to human existence. There was no power greater than the control of the State and government and their laws that had the supremacy to create fear in us. We had no purpose in life, other than get through it with as few setbacks as possible. We had no knowledge about a Higher Power or spirituality. Anything transcendental, metaphysical and supernatural was considered primitive and replaced by materialism, secularism, and a scientific outlook on nature.

This goal was achieved by eradicating all religions in the U.S.S.R. Where did it leave me personally? What did I believe? Until this conversation with Sara and despite my life in Israel and now in America, I was a product of my upbringing. Nevertheless, I also had a sixth sense, an intuition, a feeling, an *inner voice* many times whispering that there should be more than this dry pragmatism for this world. I just never let myself have the luxury of exploration into this unfamiliar subject.

Sara was one of the most unusual people in my life. She spent her life searching for the truth for herself in the area of Jewish philosophy and mysticism, but also in the other religious teachings and philosophies. She read a lot in a quest for knowledge and discoveries for herself and formed very original ideas combining a mixture of things that appeal to her strong soul. She was probably the only person that I met at that time who created her own understanding and interesting interpretations of spirituality from the pool of knowledge and didn't follow the common path. It was natural for her to understand *Kabbalah*, for example, without the confusion that I would have in my later pursuit. She was a very private person and didn't share much, but for some reason, felt a necessity to share some of her thoughts with me. The most important gift that I got from her was permission to explore this new world unknown to me, to open my mind, and to embark on my own quest into the splendid world of the infinity.

Very gradually, I started my own quiet prayers. I didn't feel so isolated and lonely in this cold world anymore. I was thanking *Elohim* for my blessings, for my beautiful children, for my family, for leading me through the many obstacles of my life, and for the music inside of me that was still alive despite the tragedy of losing my Beloved. I prayed for help in finding a way to stay in America and to bring my family here.

And when Mark and I finally got our H1 visas in the middle of March I thanked *Elohim* for all the help that had been given to us.

It was a triumphant feeling to be able to achieve our goal. We called home and let everyone know our positive news.

Lala had tons of work to do to prepare the family for the big move. Now it was her task to act alone in order to sell our apartments, our cars, our furniture, to get visas for everyone, to pack and also watch over four children at the same time. Our parents were very helpful and did everything possible to support her, but my sister was the driving force. I hurried up and sent them the tickets for the second week of May, which was a mistake on my part, since I left Lala with very limited time for the whole ordeal. I should have consulted with her first, but I was too anxious and impassioned, and it put even more pressure on my sister.

She met her responsibility with vigor and strength that was unprecedented. Despite the limited time, she became a driving force, organizing the move of the two families from one country to another. Many years later, I heard that in America, moving to a new place is considered to be one of the top stressors ever experienced in people's lives. Well, my sister performed her part graciously and efficiently. My elderly parents and four children were on her shoulders as she was making all the arrangements, selling our apartment, cars, furniture, and gathering all the necessary papers together. Mark and I truly appreciated her valiant effort, but unfortunately could not help her in her task. It became my sister's time to shine.

CHAPTER FIFTY-TWO

Meanwhile, I had one more hurdle to clear. In order for me to receive an official H1 visa, my visitor's visa from Israel had to be current. But by this time, it was expired. So my lawyer called and told me to immediately get on a plane and go to Vancouver, Canada, to extend my visa. He explained to me the simple procedure at the USA consulate in Canada, which would take just a short visit in the morning.

I had never traveled by myself in my life. Canada, in my mind, was excruciatingly cold in wintertime, the same as Russia. I had no winter clothes, coming from Israel. I bought an airline ticket for the next morning, called Joyce, telling her that I need to ask somebody from her family to drive me to the airport. Then I called my friends asking them to bring me some warm clothes. By the evening, I got a few articles of clothing in all different shapes and colors. In the morning, I dressed up and as I was looking at myself in the mirror, I realized that I looked ridiculous: long brown boots, a winter coat with some reddish foxy collar, and a strange hat of a different color. I had no time to dwell on it and went straight to the airport. We landed in Vancouver, and I felt very apprehensive looking around at the well-dressed crowd. Apparently, the weather in Vancouver was very warm and no one was dressed in winter clothing.

Going through customs was an easy task for me because I didn't have to talk, and the line was moving very fast. The officer took my passport, and as I was ready to grab it back I saw a strange look on his face. Suddenly, he got up and directed me to a separate room and asked me to follow him. My legs almost gave away.

"What is going on?" I asked. He told me to sit down and wait.

My heart was racing, but my head was empty. I had no clue what I had done wrong, other than being dressed like a clown or maybe even like a prostitute. *But that wasn't a crime in Canada*, I thought. In a little while, a different officer, very tall, blond and handsome, came into the room and sat across from me at the desk, looking at me very suspiciously. *What is going on?* I was panicky and baffled by this turn of events.

First, he asked me some formal question about my name, birth and then looking straight into my face, he asked,

"Are you trying to sneak into our country without a visa?" I looked at him in complete confusion;

"What visa, without what visa?"

"Aren't you an Israeli citizen?"

"Yes, I am, officer," I answered with my heart pounding and racing now faster and faster.

"Don't you know that as an Israeli citizen, you have to have a visa to enter Canada? We can't let you enter our country. You have to go back."

Back where? I thought, astonished. My American visa is expired, so they would not let me enter the U.S.A. either. *Oh, my God!!*

My brain was working in high gear. *What should I do now? What to say and how to explain? Why did my lawyer, to whom I paid good money, not tell me that there could be a problem? According to the Canadian officials, after all my progress and being so close to reaching my goal, I have just to go back to Israel? They expect me just to agree with them, to be a good girl, in my unfortunate situation, just to surrender all my achievements and follow their law and leave the office quietly? Sorry, Officer, I made a mistake and I am ready to leave you in your safe country and not to cause you any more problems this morning?*

Instead, I collected myself, looked straight into his eyes, and said in my broken English with my heavy Russian accent,

"Sorry, Officer, but I am not leaving the airport, and I am not going home." He looked at me, surprised, and said,

"According to the law of Canada, you absolutely cannot enter our country either, no further discussions."

It was my turn to come up with a solution. Very convincingly and strongly, I told the officer that I have to enter Canada only for one day, and I showed him my return ticket.

"All I need in Canada is to go to the American Consulate the next morning, show all my papers from my lawyer, and get the extension for my visa to go back to America." I told him that I am not some kind of spy, and I don't have any ulterior motives.

"Please, Officer, just give me a temporary visa for twelve hours, and if I don't leave on time, then my arrest would be absolutely justified."

He listened to me very attentively, and then looked at me one more time. I have no idea what his impression was of this young lady with her rambling speech. I just thought this probably wasn't happening often on his watch. A Jewish Russian Israeli with no American visa trying to enter Canada? I didn't know whether to cry or to smile. He left the room with a very confused face.

I waited for a long while, but when he came back he said,

"OK, we have decided to give you a temporary visa for twelve hours with all the consequences attached to it." He started to fill out the forms and I was rapidly thinking;

What if I spend more time in the consulate and wouldn't be able to come back on time? Then I would be in a real trouble.

"Officer," I said with a little chutzpa, "I think twenty-four hours actually would be better for me to avoid any complications." He looked at me, puzzled, and wrote "24" in the appropriate spot and smiled at me for the first time.

When I finally got outside, the weather was warm and sunny, the grass was really green, and the sky was bright and blue. There were no signs of the Russian wintery snow that I expected. I hailed a taxi and went to my hotel exhausted and hungry, but happy.

As I was sitting in the restaurant ordering my dinner, I felt so much out of my comfort zone, alone in this unknown country with Canadians all around me. Do single people really live like this, traveling alone, going to eat alone, going to the movies or concerts alone, and going home alone? It seemed to me so unnatural and sad. It was painful to think about all the single people who don't have a companion or partner in life, but I had to brush those thoughts aside, if only just for this evening.

The next morning, I was one of the first people to enter in the consulate. I got my number and was waiting for the call. I was in anguish, with my heavy heart palpitating, waiting for my turn and not knowing what exactly they would ask me and whether I would be able to answer correctly. My number was called out, and I came to the big window with a short male agent behind it. I gave him all my papers, and he asked a whole bunch of normal bureaucratic questions.

I was finally starting to breathe more easily, when suddenly his next question cut through the air like a knife.

"Mrs. Okun, according to the rules of the 'guest visa' that you got in Israel and entered into the USA with, you had no right to look for a job. You, instead, found a job and applied for a special H1 visa. Don't you know that this is against the laws of immigration?" He finished his tirade, glaring at me victoriously, gloating over the defeat of one more illegal immigrant. I wasn't sure what his role was, to give me the necessary stamp in my passport or to try to decline my petition. He was absolutely right about the facts of my situation, but I had to come up with a convincing explanation to win him over. I have had many pivotal moments in my life, but usually, I was just a pawn in the game, and the outcome did not depend on my own answers.

I didn't have time to evaluate the possibilities of trying different approaches with him to see which one would work. So, I looked at the pale, indifferent man behind the window, and my heart stopped in the anticipation of my own voice. And then in the next minute, to my own surprise, I heard myself talking assertively, and even aggressively.

"Sir, the truth of the matter is that I didn't look for a job but the private school that applied for the H1 visa was looking for ME or somebody with my qualifications. And apparently, I was the only one that had all of it. I have a Master's Degree in music from the Soviet Union, but I am also a very unique specialist in the area of early childhood musical education and developments, sir, from Israel. I am multilingual, specializing in a rare European Dalcroze method and Karl Orff's musical system for preschool-age children. Apparently, my area of expertise is almost unknown in the U.S.A and Canada, and that is why this particular private school was looking for *ME*."

He slowly lifted his eyes from the reading my papers and looked at me, perplexed, from above his glasses with a little surprise, and even curiosity. This was obviously an unusual case for him. Most of his clients were rare specialists in science, medicine, or architecture — high caliber uniqueness. And here I am, trying to become part of the elite? There was a long pause before he reached for the heavy stamp as I was watching him, mortified, afraid to breathe. Next came the most victorious moment of my life. He stamped my passport, gave it and all the rest of my papers back to me, and simply said:

"Good luck, young lady. NEXT…"

I wanted to jump and scream and dance and sing. I felt like I suddenly had wings. I looked at this man-angel with the utmost appreciation I ever felt in my heart, smiled to him, said, "Sir, thank you so, so much!" and flew out of this big and dark office to the bright sunny streets of Vancouver. *Oh, my God! I did it!!*

My dear Sergei, my Beloved, I did it!! Thank you so much for convincing me to take this course of Eurhythmic in Israel so many years ago. Who would have believed that it would make such a huge difference in my life?

In this moment, I knew that now my victorious exit from Canada would happen on time.

The triumphant feeling of personal victory against all odds stayed with my happy spirit all the way back to my new homeland called America. For the first time, I felt that the door was open for my family and me to stay and live in this great country. I made my dream come true, and I treasured this new reality with a soaring spirit, elation, joyful music in my soul and tears of happiness in my eyes. By now, I could freely thank God for walking with me hand in hand and paving the way through a complicated maze of the roads of my life.

I could not stop smiling all through my flight home and my arrival, that was so ordinary to all the rest of the passengers, but was uniquely victorious for me with such a grand feeling of great accomplishment. I stepped onto American soil with the same feeling, probably, as when Neil Armstrong stepped on the moon. *Wow!* After all, my family and I had the right to become Americans!   *Wow!!* **Wow!!!**

∞

Back at Joyce's house after all the celebration, congratulations, *Mazel Tovs*, toasts and *L'chaim*, I was telling this story with laughter and tears. I was glad that it was over. But I went to my lawyer the following day very upset, and let him know that he didn't prepare me for all those complications. My lawyer was very lawyerly looking — young, successful, rich, very handsome, very efficient. He had an executive office in downtown Palo Alto. I was in awe every time I entered his office. This gentleman was so highly educated and knew all the necessary laws of this great country. I had a lot of respect for him and appreciation for his help.

But not this time. I was really upset with him, and I let him know it. After telling him about my Canadian adventure and giving my papers back to him, I asked,

"*WHY* didn't you prepare me for the inquisition I had to endure in this situation?" His answer was, "I just sent one of my clients from Sweden on the same route, and he didn't have any problems. Sorry, I didn't realize the difference between other countries and Israel."

Oh, well, what could I add to this remark?? How could he have been so naïve as to compare Israel to any other country in the world?

CHAPTER FIFTY-THREE

Mark and I were waiting excitedly for the arrival of our families in May, 1981. They flew to New York to stay with Harold for a few days and then on to San Francisco. We both were on the verge of ecstasy in expectation of hugging everyone and welcoming them into our new home in America. When the passengers started to come out of the narrow corridor one by one, I had a hard time keeping myself from running inside against the current.

A few moments later, the whole family came into the terminal right into our waiting arms. It was a moment of real joy for all of us, but a confusing moment for our children. They had grown up so much during this year and had lived through so many changes. Anat was much taller, beautiful with her dark hair and blue eyes, but as happy as she was to see me again, I saw a lot of sadness in her eyes that I hadn't seen before. I felt that Jacob had forgotten me a little bit and was surprised to see me again. My father looked much sicker and skinnier, but had a happy smile on his face. My sister looked great despite a very difficult year. I couldn't stop hugging my mother. Mark's children Misha and Avi looked surprised and excited to see their Abba again. Everyone was in shock, but thrilled to finally be reunited.

Our families started a new journey of discovery in the country of my dreams. I understood that Anechka didn't want to leave Israel, which she loved so much, and didn't want to come and to live in America. I had long conversations with her trying to explain that when she turned eighteen, she could go back and study and live in Israel. In the meantime we had to adjust to our circumstances and rebuilt our family life in a new country.

At this point in my life, I have lived in America for the longest part of my life. It has been a challenging and in many ways an unexpectedly complicated journey. In my first years in America, I was endlessly surprised about how people of this country feel that they live on a separate planet, disconnected from the rest of the world without trying to understand it. I celebrated when I heard Reagan finally calling the U.S.S.R. by its deserved name, "An Evil Empire." But still, many Americans disagreed. Maybe America would like to be separated from the world, but the world was coming in the back door to disturb America. I felt that Americans didn't see it coming and continued living unprepared.

When I finally studied some of American history and the Constitution, I was astounded by the pure genius of the Founding Fathers and their deep understanding of human nature in creating the best possible system for human co-existence. *"We, the people"* was a 360-degree turn away from the rotten Soviet system, created by the communists.

But socialists always use the greatest appealing words to inflame the masses for the illusion of a better future. They always make many empty promises that couldn't possibly come true. But the masses want to believe the propaganda, and refuse to see the truth. Those fallacious ideas of utopia from previous generations are making their way back into the 21st century as new ideas. Many Americans, especially from the younger generation, are enthusiastically traveling the roads that have been traveled before so tragically and unsuccessfully.

Unfortunately, it is easy to lose freedom when you don't treasure it and are not ready to fight and die for it. The greatest treasure of the U.S.A is its Constitution and my hope is that these new generations will study history more and will be able to realize the importance of preserving this jewel. But sometimes, I feel that humanity is just going around in circles, despite the unbelievable advances in technology.

Toward the sunset of my life, I don't want to see history repeating itself. I am witnessing many signs of renewed socialism and I fear ending up in circumstances similar to those in Russia, where my life's journey began many years ago. I am always praying that it will never happen in this country, which has been so richly blessed by God.

∞

In some paradoxical way, those of us who lived in the communist system with the illusion of equality were dreaming about freedom and liberty and it seems to me that some portion of Americans who have freedom and liberty are dreaming of equality. And my heart is screaming to them. "There is no *equality*, but only *slavery*, but the Constitution in America promises us *freedom* and *liberty*."

Fight for your freedom, because it can easily slip away if you don't!

Treasure the freedom of speech. I see that it is slipping away, and fear of being politically incorrect is entering the hearts and minds of the people more and more. Fear is the first step on the road of losing freedom. Political correctness has become a household reality and is spreading like a cancer all through the nation. It will stay permanently if not eradicated at the beginning stages. For the young generation it could become the norm, and they would have no idea of what has been lost. This is another road to slavery.

The *slave-master* tells you what you should say and what you shouldn't. The next step is what you should think and what you shouldn't. Is history going to repeat itself, just without the red colors?

Fight for your freedom, because it is easy to lose if you don't!

CHAPTER FIFTY-FOUR

I have returned to Israel a few times for visits and was amazed by the changes in this great country. At some point, common sense triumphed, and the Israelis have changed their course to a more capitalistic system, away from the absurdities of socialism with all its hardship. In many ways, the country is almost unrecognizable. There is so much free enterprise and innovation now. The advances in technology, medicine, science, agriculture, and education are staggering. This is where the Jewish people, working together to create their beautiful country, are at their best. But they have many unsolved political problems and very complicated relationships with the neighboring countries. Despite it all, the most amazing quality that Israelis have is to *"Choose Life"* and to live every day fully with no fear of tomorrow, no matter what. I feel the grace of God all around this Holy Land, but especially in Jerusalem.

My children, grandchildren and I, together with Sergei's brother Victor and his family, went to the cemetery to visit Sergei. It was a real moment of silence and reflection for all of us with a lot of sadness, sorrow, and grief. I took some time later to be with Sergei alone, and with tears in my eyes and a smile on my lips, I shared the deepest feelings of my spiritual connection with my Beloved and my love for him, which I would carry in my heart for the rest of my life. At the same time, I felt a sense of pride in presenting to Sergei my biggest accomplishment — our thriving, grown up children and their families. "I didn't drop the ball, Sergei. I truly did the best I could under the circumstances."

By the end of 1991, the U.S.S.R. ceased to exist. Dissolution of the Soviet Empire created independent republics and a temporary illusion of the end of the Cold War.

I never had any desire to go back to my so-called "homeland" for even a brief visit. But Jacob, my son, after finishing college, wanted to see the place of his family origins. I decided to satisfy his curiosity and to show him the reality of the country that brought so much tragedy to life of millions of people, including his family.

Maybe I also falsely hoped to see some settled changes, some progress, fresh air and some new energy. And I recognized some new little steps for the better, mostly that there were no more lines to buy things, and food was plentiful, although very expensive. But at the same time, I felt the same way as before I left. Mistrust, gloom and doom were still there, and the life of the people hadn't changed much.

It was painful to stand in the front of our apartment in Leningrad and realize how much the conditions were unchanged — poverty-stricken, meager and deprived. I think Jacob was utterly shocked. It would be hard for him to imagine a worse place for his Mama and his Aunt Lala to grow up in. It brought a lot of emotional memories back to me, both happy and sad. I was humbled. I spent 20 years of my life in this sentimental, but disturbing "hell-hole." *Wow!* Being children, we didn't have anything to compare our living conditions with, and so we didn't realize how disadvantaged and destitute we were. We just didn't know any better.

In my opinion, there is no hope for the world that I ran away from. I couldn't wait to leave. I never believed in the finality of the end of the Cold War. The Russians just put on the brakes for a while to regroup. The leaders are thirsty for power and domination in the world, and nostalgic for the days of Stalin. The Cold War years were the days of Russian superiority, and they allowed Russians to feel pride and unbelievable patriotism. Maybe out of their own inferiority complex, they strived for greatness in the wrong bullish way. The "Collective Image" is still so much more important than any individual achievements. And Mother–Russia still demands all the sacrifices from little insignificant people for its "Deserved Glory." They always will find ways to blame America for all their problems, creating a new circle of "justifiable hate." I couldn't wait to get out of my unfortunate place of birth, never to come back again.

∞

In my personal life, I have discovered many sides to human nature that were unknown to me before. It was much easier for me to see the enemies of happiness that were outside of us. But I came to the conclusion that there are enemies of happiness even stronger inside of us, in our minds, which create a real struggle not only between societies and countries, but also between and within people.

I am more and more fascinated by the science of the complicated human mind. Real progress in medicine has been made with advances in the area of heart disease and I am sure the doctors could have saved Sergei easily with all the new technology available now. But in the area of the mind, the doctors are still in the dark ages. Hopefully, progress will be made soon in this area, too. I have witnessed many people suffering in the U.S.A. because of endless disorders that I was unaware of in the past. These are souls tormented within themselves who can experience real unhappiness, even in the best country in the world. My wish is that solutions will be found in this 21st century to help all these unfortunate people.

I have experienced a clash of civilizations during my long marriage to my American husband. Robert grew up on the opposite end of the spectrum from me in a wealthy environment in Hollywood, California. I had a journey of crucial discoveries on this roller-coaster ride of adjustments to the new realities of my life. Our beautiful American daughter Natalie was born in 1986 and gave us a lot of pleasure plus a lot of soul-searching about bringing up a child in this free society.

My three children were born in three different countries, on two different continents. It is an amazing road of discovery to watch their lives unfold.

And above all, watching the seven grandchildren of Sergei and I growing up in this beautiful country is such a treasure and blessing from God. I see Sergei living in our children and grandchildren; I feel his connection to us all. I feel his presence during happy moments, graduation ceremonies or weddings of his children, or proudly watching the

Bar-Mitzvah of Anat and Aviv's son Elliot or their daughter Chantal's dance recital. I feel him smiling as Jacob's twins were born this year and Jacob and Monica's effort to raise five children, all under the age of seven, with both of them working full-time jobs! And all the times I feel heartfelt gratitude to God for all those blessings and for making my life possible. What an unbelievable journey it is...

All through my life, I also was incredibly fortunate to meet or come across so many remarkable people who enriched my own life experience in so many different ways. Many of them became very close friends. Some of them I see every week and some I haven't seen in years. We live in different countries, or in different states. I treasure the connections, the battles of ideas, the closeness of hearts and minds, the warmth, and the love. I thank God for letting me become acquainted with all those people. I think God is watching me with a smile — by the end of the day, so to speak, I have had a great human experience.

Robert and I have traveled the world together and that has been a highlight of my life. We live on a beautiful planet and we must learn to appreciate the variety in our lives, styles, religions, culture and ideas. My hope is that one day we as a people will be able to learn from history and not to repeat the mistakes of the past, to learn somehow to co-exist in peace despite all the odds. Only then the lives of the previous generations would not have lived in vain.

CPSIA information can be obtained at www.ICGtesting.com
Printed in the USA
LVOW07s0531130815

449752LV00002B/153/P